The Ultimate Guide to Finding Your Life's Purpose

The Comprehensive Manual to Life's Most Profound Question

Author – Stan Barren

Brought to you by InspirationDB

Stan Barren

Legal and Copyright Disclaimer

The author and publisher shall in no event be held liable to any party for any direct, indirect, punitive, special, incidental, or other consequential damages arising directly or indirectly from any use of this material, which is provided "as is", and without warranties.

Table of Contents

Stan Barren

Introduction

In the bustling cacophony of life, amidst the endless to-do lists, obligations, and the relentless pursuit of success, there's a profound question that whispers to us all: "Why am I here?" This isn't merely a philosophical musing or a late-night contemplation, but a deep-rooted, intrinsic quest to understand our place in this vast universe.

The Ultimate Guide to Finding Your Life's Purpose isn't just another self-help manual; it's a journey, a map that guides you towards that elusive 'north star', the purpose that lights up your life's path.

From ancient philosophers gazing at the heavens to the modern individual scrolling through inspirational quotes on a screen, the question of purpose has been a constant. It is intertwined with our sense of self, our motivations, our choices, and, most importantly, our happiness.

Yet, finding one's life purpose is not about achieving a singular monumental goal or reaching a predetermined destination. Instead, it's about alignment—a harmony between who you are, what you do, and how you impact the world.

As we navigate the chapters of this book, we will unravel layers, debunk myths, and embark on introspective exercises, all aiming to unveil the purpose that perhaps lies dormant within.

It's a journey of discovery, of embracing the vastness of possibilities, and ultimately, finding the unique melody that resonates with your soul.

This guide doesn't promise an overnight revelation. Instead, it offers tools, insights, and a compass to navigate the terrains of self-awareness, exploration, and alignment.

Whether you're in the throes of a mid-life crisis, at a crossroads in your career, or simply curious, this book aims to be the beacon guiding you towards understanding your life's deeper calling.

Importance of Having A Life's Purpose

Life's purpose is often described as the overarching theme or direction that gives one's life meaning, guiding our choices and actions in a cohesive manner. Its significance is multifaceted, deeply rooted both in our psychological makeup and our sociocultural needs. At the most basic level, having a purpose acts as a compass, providing clarity in moments of confusion or doubt.

When faced with challenging decisions, understanding our core motivations can illuminate the path most aligned with our inner values and aspirations. This clarity often translates to increased motivation, as knowing 'why' we're doing something provides the drive to push through obstacles.

Beyond decision-making, a defined purpose is intrinsically linked to one's well-being and mental health. Studies have consistently shown that individuals with a clear sense of purpose report higher levels of happiness, satisfaction, and even longevity. They often experience lower levels of stress, anxiety, and depression.

This is because purpose anchors us, giving life a sense of continuity and coherence amidst its inevitable chaos. When the going gets tough, as it invariably does, having a purpose can be the life raft that keeps one afloat, the reminder that there's a bigger picture we're contributing to.

From a societal standpoint, purpose-driven individuals often engage more proactively within their communities, driven by the need to contribute positively to the world around them.

They are more likely to partake in voluntary work, charitable activities, and community outreach, acting as pivotal members in societal development.

Furthermore, in a world overflowing with choices and distractions, having a guiding purpose can act as a filter, helping one allocate time and resources more efficiently, making decisions that resonate with one's overarching goals.

In essence, possessing a clear life's purpose is not merely a philosophical luxury but a vital component for holistic well-being. It offers direction, enhances mental health, and fosters a sense of belonging, making it indispensable in the quest for a fulfilled life.

Case Study Illustrating the Transformative Power of Purpose

Anika's Journey to Purpose

Anika had always been an excellent student. From high school to college, her report cards were a series of A's, and her extracurricular activities showcased a student engaged with her community. On paper, she was poised for success.

Following a path seemingly predestined by her grades and the expectations of those around her, she took up a job at a high-profile law firm right after graduating from a top-tier law school. The pay check was enviable, the prestige unmistakable. Yet, every morning, as she donned her tailored suits, a sense of emptiness lingered.

One day, during a pro bono case for a low-income family fighting for their home, Anika experienced a profound shift. As she listened to their story, she was deeply moved by their resilience, love for one another, and the community that rallied around them.

This was the first time in her professional life where she felt genuinely connected to her work. It dawned on her that while she had been chasing a predefined notion of success, her heart was yearning for purpose—making a real difference in the lives of others.

This realization prompted Anika to reassess her career trajectory. She decided to leave her high-paying job and founded a non-profit organization dedicated to providing legal assistance to marginalized communities.

The work was challenging, and the pay was a fraction of what she used to earn, but the fulfilment she felt was unparalleled.

No longer were her days marked by monotonous paperwork; they were now filled with stories of lives changed and communities uplifted. Anika had discovered her purpose, and it transformed not just her career but her entire life. She felt more connected, passionate, and alive than ever before.

This journey underscored a universal truth: success, when detached from purpose, can often feel hollow. On the contrary, when one aligns with their true purpose, even challenges become stepping stones, and work transforms into a labor of love.

Chapter 1: Understanding Purpose

In the vast expanse of human existence, one question has perennially haunted our thoughts and kindled our imaginations: "Why am I here?" At the intersection of this question lies a single, powerful concept: purpose.

It's a word we hear often, a concept many seek relentlessly, and a journey that all of us, knowingly or unknowingly, embark upon. Yet, what does 'purpose' truly mean? How does it differ from the passions that ignite our enthusiasm or the professions that define our societal roles?

In this chapter, we will delve deep into the essence of purpose. We'll dissect its layers, revealing its significance in the grand tapestry of life. We'll distinguish it from the adjacent concepts that often blur its understanding.

By the end of this exploration, you'll not only have a clearer notion of what purpose means but also a foundational understanding that will guide you as you journey through the subsequent chapters. So, let's begin our quest to comprehend this pivotal pillar of human existence: purpose.

Definition of 'Purpose'

The term 'purpose' holds a profound and multidimensional meaning, often intricately woven into the fabric of our individual and collective experiences. At its core, purpose refers to the reason for which something is done, created, or exists.

It is a compass, an intrinsic motivation that provides direction, shaping our actions, decisions, and aspirations. Purpose isn't just about achieving a particular end but is more about understanding one's role in the vast tapestry of life.

From an existential standpoint, purpose delves deep into the questions of 'why are we here?' and 'what is the meaning of life?'. These questions, as ancient as humanity itself, have led countless individuals on philosophical, spiritual, and introspective journeys.

But beyond these larger life questions, purpose also manifests in the everyday. It is present in the career paths we choose, the relationships we nurture, and the causes we champion.

In a psychological context, purpose can be seen as a crucial component of a fulfilling life. It lends a sense of coherence to our experiences, providing a narrative that connects our past, present, and future.

This narrative isn't just a lofty ideal; it has tangible benefits, grounding us during tumultuous times and elevating our most joyous moments.

However, it's vital to recognize that purpose is deeply personal. What offers purpose to one person might seem insignificant to another. It's a culmination of one's values, beliefs, passions, and life experiences.

While societal norms or external pressures may attempt to dictate or influence our purpose, true purpose resonates at an individual level, echoing with clarity and conviction in the chambers of one's heart.

The Difference Between Purpose, Passion, And Profession

Purpose

Definition: At its core, purpose refers to the profound reason or motivation behind our actions, decisions, and life choices. It is the overarching theme or direction in life that provides us with a sense of meaning and fulfilment.

- Innate: Purpose often feels innate and intrinsic to who we are. It's a guiding compass that remains relatively stable throughout life, even if how we express it might change.
- Beyond Self: Purpose often transcends individual desires or ambitions, connecting us to something larger—be it community, spirituality, or a greater cause.
- Fulfilment: Living with purpose ensures a deeper sense of satisfaction and contentment, as actions align with one's core values and beliefs.

Passion

Definition: Passion is an intense enthusiasm or desire for something. It's that burning zeal or fervor we feel for activities, subjects, or pursuits that resonate deeply with us.

- Emotion-driven: Unlike the steady guidance of purpose, passion is more volatile, often fuelled by strong emotions and can ebb and flow.

- Individualistic: Passions tend to be more personal and self-centric. They are activities or pursuits that bring individual joy, excitement, or satisfaction.

- Motivating Force: Passion acts as a powerful motivator, pushing individuals to pursue what they love, sometimes even against odds. It's the fire that drives action.

- Evolution: As individuals grow and experience life, passions can change, evolve, or even be replaced by new ones.

Profession

Definition: Profession pertains to one's career or job—the formal work or service one provides in exchange for compensation, recognition, or livelihood.

- Economic Aspect: Unlike purpose (intrinsic) and passion (emotion-driven), a profession is closely tied to economic necessities, providing a means for livelihood and financial stability.

- Skill-Based: Professions often require specific skills, training, or education. It's where one's competencies are honed and applied.

- Not Always Aligned: While the ideal scenario is for one's profession to align with their passion and purpose, this isn't always the case.

Many people have professions unrelated to their passions or purpose.

- Societal Role: A profession often defines an individual's role in society, giving them an identity based on their work or contributions.

In an ideal world, these three converge, where an individual's purpose is expressed through their passion and manifested in their profession.

However, the distinct differences between them mean that they can exist independently of one another. Understanding these distinctions can help individuals make more informed life choices, ensuring greater alignment and fulfilment.

Why Having A Purpose Matters? - Benefits for Mental Health, Motivation, And Overall Well-Being

Having a sense of purpose can be likened to possessing an internal compass, guiding us through the intricacies of life. This guiding light not only helps determine our direction but also enhances the quality of the journey itself.

Delving into its profound effects, one quickly realizes that having a purpose is not a mere luxury but a necessity for our psychological, motivational, and holistic wellness.

Mental Health: A robust body of research suggests a direct correlation between possessing a clear purpose in life and better mental health outcomes. Purpose acts as a buffer, shielding us from life's inevitable storms and reducing the risk of conditions like depression and anxiety.

Individuals with a strong sense of purpose tend to exhibit greater resilience, enabling them to bounce back from adversities more efficiently than their counterparts.

This resilience stems from the understanding that challenges, no matter how daunting, are temporary hurdles on the path to fulfilling a greater mission. Moreover, a defined purpose also provides a sense of belonging and connectivity, drastically reducing feelings of isolation and loneliness. When life gets overwhelming, knowing that there's a larger reason behind our existence can be the anchor that keeps us grounded.

Motivation: Purpose is the fuel that ignites our intrinsic motivation. When actions and tasks are aligned with a broader purpose, they transform from being mundane chores to passionate pursuits.

This intrinsic motivation, steered by purpose, is sustainable and self-renewing. It propels individuals to persevere in the face of obstacles, instilling a sense of dedication and commitment.

The clarity that comes with understanding one's purpose ensures that individuals aren't merely drifting through life but are propelled forward by a compelling vision of what they want to achieve.

This drive often translates into higher productivity, better focus, and an unwavering determination to overcome barriers in the path to one's goals.

Overall Well-Being: Beyond mental health and motivation, having a purpose contributes to a holistic sense of well-being. Physiologically, a life driven by purpose is often linked to lower cortisol levels, better cardiovascular health, and a generally enhanced immune system. This is likely due to the reduced stress levels and more positive outlook associated with having meaningful life goals.

Furthermore, purposeful living is often synonymous with a deeper sense of satisfaction and contentment. It offers a clearer perspective, helping individuals prioritize their time and resources, leading to a more balanced and fulfilling life.

Those who understand and live their purpose tend to cultivate better relationships, as their interactions are imbued with intent and meaning. They also often report a deeper sense of contentment and happiness, as they recognize their role in the larger tapestry of life.

In conclusion, purpose is not merely about identifying our life's work or defining our legacy. It's about enriching every facet of our existence. In the journey of life, where uncertainties are the only certainty, having a purpose can be the most reliable map, ensuring that every step, even if meandering, is a step forward.

Chapter 2: Historical and Cultural Perspectives on Purpose

Throughout the ages, mankind has grappled with the profound question: "Why are we here?" The quest for purpose is as old as human civilization itself, transcending borders, cultures, and eras.

Every society, from ancient civilizations to modern cultures, has sought to understand and define the purpose of life. This pursuit has not only been a personal endeavor but has shaped the philosophies, traditions, and ideologies of entire cultures.

In this chapter, we will embark on a fascinating journey across time and space, exploring how different cultures and historical epochs have approached the concept of purpose.

From the ancient Greeks pondering their place in the cosmos, to indigenous tribes finding purpose in their connection to the land and spirits, to Eastern philosophies that view purpose as a path to enlightenment. each perspective offers a unique lens through which we can better understand our own individual quests for meaning.

By delving into these diverse viewpoints, we aim to enrich our own understanding of purpose. Recognizing that the search for meaning is a universal pursuit can be immensely comforting and illuminating.

It connects us to generations past and to people from all walks of life, reminding us that, despite our differences, the human spirit is bound by an innate desire to find purpose and meaning in existence.

How Different Cultures and Societies Define and Approach Purpose

In the vast tapestry of human civilization, the quest for purpose has been a timeless pursuit. Yet, the way we define and approach this purpose varies significantly across different cultures and societies, shaped by historical, religious, and philosophical influences.

Western Societies: In many Western societies, especially influenced by the capitalist mindset, purpose has often been linked with individual achievement and personal fulfilment.

The American Dream, for instance, is a cultural narrative tied to the idea that anyone, regardless of their background, can achieve success (often equated with financial prosperity) through hard work and determination. Thus, for many in these societies, finding one's purpose can be intimately tied to individual accomplishments, career success, and personal growth.

Eastern Societies: Contrastingly, many Eastern philosophies, deeply rooted in traditions like Confucianism, Buddhism, and Hinduism, perceive purpose through a more collective and holistic lens. For instance, in Hinduism, the concept of 'Dharma' refers to one's duty or righteous path in life, which may involve personal, social, and cosmic responsibilities.

Similarly, in Japanese culture, the idea of "ikigai" suggests a convergence of what one loves, what the world needs, what one can be paid for, and what one is good at. It's a harmonious blend of personal joy, societal contribution, and professional satisfaction.

Middle Eastern Perspectives: In the Middle East, where religions like Islam, Judaism, and Christianity have deep roots, purpose is often seen through a religious and spiritual lens.

For example, in Islamic philosophy, the idea of "Rizq" (provision or sustenance) suggests that everyone's purpose and provision are predetermined by a higher power, and humans should strive to recognize and fulfil this divine assignment.

African Cultures: Many African cultures, with their rich tapestry of traditions and beliefs, view purpose from the standpoint of community and interconnectedness. The Southern African philosophy of "Ubuntu" encapsulates this beautifully.

Often translated as "I am because we are," Ubuntu emphasizes communal values, mutual respect, and shared responsibility. Purpose, in such societies, often intertwines with serving one's community and contributing to its well-being.

Indigenous Cultures: For many indigenous cultures around the world, purpose is deeply rooted in their connection to the land, the ancestors, and the larger cosmos.

The Aboriginal cultures of Australia, for instance, derive purpose and meaning through their Dreamtime stories, which are both creation myths and guiding moral tales. These narratives provide a framework for understanding one's place in the world and responsibilities towards it.

While the intrinsic human desire to find purpose remains a universal constant, the paths we tread in this quest are profoundly shaped by our cultural and societal contexts.

Understanding these diverse perspectives can enrich our own journey, allowing us to draw from a broader palette of ideas and beliefs in our search for meaning.

Philosophers and Thinkers on The Topic of Life's Purpose

Socrates (c. 469 – 399 BC)

Socrates, the classical Greek philosopher, is best remembered for his dedication to the pursuit of self-knowledge. He often stated, "The unexamined life is not worth living." For Socrates, the purpose of life was internal, philosophical reflection.

Through continuous self-examination and the Socratic method of questioning, one could reach a deeper understanding of their own nature and, by extension, the nature of the universe. Life's purpose, in his view, was to live with virtue and wisdom.

Aristotle (384 – 322 BC)

For the ancient Greek philosopher Aristotle, the purpose or "final cause" of an individual's life is eudaimonia, often translated as "happiness" or "flourishing." Aristotle believed that each individual has a particular function or "ergon" that, when fulfilled, leads to eudaimonia.

This fulfilment doesn't just relate to pleasures or material gains but is deeply rooted in living according to reason and virtue. For Aristotle, life's purpose is to live a life of rational activity in accordance with virtue.

Albert Camus (1913-1960)

In the 20th century, existentialist philosopher Albert Camus grappled with the concept of the absurd—the clash between our desire for purpose and the seemingly indifferent universe.

In his essay "The Myth of Sisyphus," Camus suggests that even in the face of the absurd, one can still find individual meaning. While he believed the universe does not inherently have a purpose, he argued that we can still live authentically by rebelling against the absurd and embracing life's experiences.

Friedrich Nietzsche (1844-1900)

Nietzsche, a prominent figure in existentialist thought, believed that traditional sources of purpose, like religion, had lost their power in the modern age.

In "Thus Spoke Zarathustra," he introduced the idea of the Übermensch (or Overman) – a person who creates their own values and purpose in the absence of traditional ones.

Nietzsche posited that one should strive to overcome oneself, creating individual purpose in a world that might otherwise seem devoid of any.

Viktor Frankl (1905 – 1997)

Frankl, a neurologist, psychiatrist, and Holocaust survivor, developed a therapeutic approach known as logotherapy. His work, "Man's Search for Meaning," details his experiences in concentration camps and his subsequent development of logotherapy.

Frankl believed that the primary human drive is not pleasure, as Freud suggested, but the pursuit of what we find meaningful. He posited that life has meaning under all circumstances, even the most miserable ones, and it's up to individuals to uncover that meaning. Through struggles and suffering, one can find purpose and meaning.

Jean-Paul Sartre (1905 – 1980)

The French existentialist philosopher Jean-Paul Sartre held that existence precedes essence, which means that one first exists and then defines their own essence or purpose. In a universe without a predetermined purpose or cosmic order, humans are radically free and responsible for their own actions.

This freedom, however, comes with the burden of choice. Each person must, according to Sartre, create their own purpose and meaning in life. This act of self-creation and responsibility is what he termed "bad faith," where individuals can either confront and embrace their freedom or flee from it.

Immanuel Kant (1724-1804)

A central figure in modern philosophy, Kant believed in a moral universe where reason dictates the purpose of life. For him, life's purpose was not about personal happiness or pleasure. Instead, it was about fulfilling our duties and obligations, which he outlined in his "Categorical Imperative."

By this principle, one's actions should be guided by moral laws that can be universally applied, ensuring that we treat others as ends in themselves and not merely as means to our ends.

Confucius (551-479 BCE)

Moving to Eastern philosophy, Confucius, a Chinese philosopher, taught that the purpose of life was to live morally and ethically. This was to be achieved through the cultivation of virtues, respect for traditions, and proper social relationships.

For Confucius, living in harmony with society, family, and oneself was the key to a purposeful life. His teachings, known as Confucianism, have deeply influenced Chinese culture and thought for over two millennia.

Siddhartha Gautama, The Buddha (c. 563-483 BCE)

The Buddha's teachings revolved around the alleviation of suffering and the attainment of enlightenment. He posited that life is characterized by suffering (Dukkha), caused primarily by desires.

The purpose of life, according to Buddhist philosophy, is to understand and break free from this cycle of suffering, eventually attaining Nirvana – a state of ultimate peace and liberation from the cycle of rebirth. This journey involves following the Eightfold Path, a set of ethical and mental practices.

Laozi (Lao Tzu, c. 6th century BCE)

The foundational figure of Daoism, Laozi is attributed with writing the "Dao De Jing" (Tao Te Ching). For Laozi, the purpose of life is found in aligning oneself with the Dao, often translated as "the Way" - an underlying principle that governs the universe.

By living in accordance with the Dao, a principle of simplicity, spontaneity, and non-contention, individuals can achieve harmony and balance. Laozi emphasized the importance of "Wu Wei," or non-action, which means acting naturally without resistance or effort, allowing life to unfold as it should.

Simone de Beauvoir (1908-1986)

An existentialist philosopher and feminist, de Beauvoir, in her work "The Ethics of Ambiguity," postulated that humans are condemned to freedom, and with this freedom comes the responsibility to create one's own purpose.

She believed that one achieves freedom and finds purpose by engaging actively with the world, taking on projects, and pursuing authentic relationships. For de Beauvoir, genuine freedom arises from understanding and embracing one's ambiguity and then acting purposefully in the world.

Martin Heidegger (1889-1976)

A significant figure in existential phenomenology, Heidegger's exploration into life's purpose was rooted in the question of "Being." In his seminal work "Being and Time," he introduced the concept of "Dasein," or "being-there," to represent human existence.

Heidegger argued that the true nature and purpose of life can be uncovered by confronting our mortality and understanding the temporality of existence. By acknowledging and embracing our "being-toward-death," we can live more authentically and find genuine meaning in our actions.

Søren Kierkegaard (1813-1855)

Often regarded as the father of existentialism, Kierkegaard believed that the individual is solely responsible for giving their own life meaning and living it authentically. He postulated that life can be lived on three levels: the aesthetic (pursuit of pleasure), the ethical (commitment to moral duty), and the religious (personal relationship with the divine).

For Kierkegaard, true purpose is found by moving beyond the aesthetic to the ethical and religious stages, engaging deeply with personal faith and moral imperatives.

Swami Vivekananda (1863-1902)

A key figure in the introduction of Indian philosophies to the Western world, Vivekananda's view on life's purpose was rooted in Vedanta. He believed that the ultimate goal of life is to realize the divine within oneself.

By practicing self-control, purity, and meditation, one can perceive the divine essence in all beings and experiences. For Vivekananda, service to humanity, seeing them as manifestations of the divine, was also a path to realizing one's life's purpose.

Rumi (1207 – 1273)

The Persian poet and Sufi mystic, Rumi, offers a spiritual take on life's purpose. His poems often speak of an intimate connection with the divine and a yearning to merge with the cosmic source.

For Rumi, life's purpose is to seek the divine, to experience love in its purest form, and to recognize the divine essence within oneself. His poetry is a testament to the inner journey of the soul seeking union and purpose in the grand dance of existence.

Chapter 3: The Science of Purpose

As we embark on our exploration of life's purpose, it's tempting to view it solely as a philosophical or spiritual quest. Historically, the question of why we exist and what our purpose is has been posed by philosophers, theologians, and thinkers who've delved deep into the human soul.

Yet, in our modern age, where empirical evidence reigns supreme, one might wonder: Can the intangible idea of "purpose" stand up to the scrutiny of science? Is there a tangible link between having a purpose and our well-being, or is it all just anecdotal?

The answer, perhaps surprisingly to some, lies at the crossroads of psychology, neuroscience, and sociology. Over the past few decades, researchers have been captivated by the profound effects of having a purpose on our mental and physical health.

From the way our brains light up in MRI scans when we engage in purposeful activities, to the measurable impact of purpose on our longevity and immune function, the evidence is compelling.

In this chapter, we'll dive deep into the scientific studies, experiments, and research that unveil the tangible benefits of having a purpose.

Through quantifiable data and intriguing experiments, we'll explore how purpose not only elevates the quality of our lives but can also, quite literally, add years to it. Prepare to be fascinated, for the science of purpose paints a picture as profound as any philosophical treatise on the subject.

Psychological and neurological studies about purpose

The connection between purpose and psychological and neurological health has garnered increasing interest over the years. Researchers have delved into understanding how purpose can impact our mental state, brain health, and overall life satisfaction.

Psychological Studies on Purpose:

From a psychological perspective, the sense of purpose is often associated with numerous positive outcomes. One of the foundational theories, Victor Frankl's "Logotherapy," posits that the primary human drive is to find meaning in life.

Frankl, a Holocaust survivor, suggested that individuals who can find meaning, even in the direst of circumstances, possess the capability to survive and thrive.

His observations were based on his experiences in concentration camps, where those with a sense of purpose seemed more resilient.

Contemporary research supports these early observations. Studies have indicated that individuals with a strong sense of purpose tend to have better mental health outcomes, including reduced rates of depression and anxiety.

They often showcase increased resilience, allowing them to bounce back from adversity more effectively. A purpose-driven life provides a shield against the existential crises and feelings of emptiness that can plague individuals, especially during challenging times.

Neurological Studies on Purpose:

On the neurological front, the relationship between purpose and brain health has been a captivating subject. One of the significant findings has been the protective role of purpose against cognitive decline.

A study from the Rush Alzheimer's Disease Canter found that individuals with a high sense of purpose had a 30% lower rate of cognitive decline compared to those with a lower sense of purpose, even when the brain showed signs of Alzheimer's-like pathology.

Furthermore, brain imaging studies have revealed that when individuals engage in purpose-driven activities or reflect on their life's meaning, there's increased activity in the prefrontal cortex, a brain region associated with executive functions, decision-making, and self-regulation.

This suggests that a strong sense of purpose might promote higher-order cognitive processes. There's also evidence to suggest that purpose can play a role in pain management.

The brain's regions responsible for pain processing, such as the anterior cingulate cortex and insula, seem to be less active in individuals with a high sense of purpose when they're exposed to painful stimuli.

This implies that having a purpose could act as a natural analgesic, reducing perceived pain levels.

Both psychological and neurological studies emphasize the profound role of purpose in shaping our mental and neurological health.

A life driven by purpose appears not only to enrich our existence with meaning but also to offer tangible benefits to our brain's functionality and health.

How Purpose Impacts Happiness, Longevity, and Stress

From time immemorial, humans have been driven by an innate desire to find purpose in life. While philosophers, poets, and thinkers have explored the profound layers of purpose, only in recent decades has science delved into the tangible impacts of living a purpose-driven life.

One might ponder: does having a defined purpose genuinely change the quality and perhaps even the length of our lives? Current research strongly suggests that the answer is a resounding 'yes'.

A clear sense of purpose not only uplifts our spirit, bringing about happiness and contentment, but it also has profound implications for our physiological well-being, influencing our lifespan and how we cope with stress.

Happiness and Purpose:

The profound relationship between purpose and happiness has been studied extensively in psychology and philosophy.

At its core, purpose acts as a compass, guiding individuals toward actions and pursuits that align with their core values and beliefs. This alignment, in turn, fuels a sense of contentment and satisfaction.

When people engage in activities that resonate with their purpose, they often experience a state of "flow," a term introduced by psychologist Mihaly Csikszentmihalyi to describe the immersion and complete absorption in what one is doing. This state not only heightens creativity and productivity but also significantly boosts happiness.

Moreover, a defined purpose can provide individuals with a broader perspective, allowing them to see past transient adversities, focusing instead on the bigger picture.

This can lead to a deeper, more sustained form of happiness, as opposed to the fleeting joy derived from momentary pleasures.

Longevity and Purpose:

The impact of purpose on longevity is another exciting facet explored in several studies, particularly in areas known as "Blue Zones" — regions where people live exceptionally long lives.

One commonality among inhabitants of these zones, spanning from Okinawa in Japan to Sardinia in Italy, is a clear sense of purpose, or what the Okinawans call "Ikigai," meaning a reason for being.

Having a reason to get up in the morning, a motivation that goes beyond just the mundane, seems to be linked to longer life expectancy.

One potential explanation is that purpose-driven individuals are more proactive about their health and well-being, making choices that support longevity.

Additionally, a strong sense of purpose may decrease the risks of degenerative diseases, as it fosters a positive outlook and reduces chronic stress.

Stress and Purpose:

Stress, in its chronic form, is known to be a precursor to multiple health issues, from cardiovascular diseases to weakened immunity. Purpose, however, can act as a buffer against stress.

When faced with challenges, individuals with a clear sense of purpose often possess an inherent resilience. They perceive obstacles not as insurmountable threats but as temporary setbacks that serve a larger narrative.

This mindset shift can drastically reduce the detrimental effects of stress. The body's physiological response to stress, which includes the release of the hormone cortisol, can be moderated when one views the stressor in the context of a larger purpose or mission.

In other words, purpose can change our stress narrative, allowing us to approach challenges with optimism and vigor rather than anxiety and trepidation.

In conclusion, a well-defined purpose not only enriches our lives with happiness and meaning but also has tangible benefits for our health and longevity.

Embracing one's purpose can transform challenges into opportunities, and in doing so, foster resilience, reduce stress, and pave the way for a longer, more fulfilled life.

Chapter 4: Common Blocks to Finding Purpose

As we embark on the intricate journey to uncover our life's purpose, it's not uncommon to encounter roadblocks along the way. These obstructions are not just mere delays but significant challenges that can often derail our quest or, at times, even make us question the very essence of our search.

Yet, understanding these blocks is just as crucial as understanding the nature of purpose itself. By recognizing what holds us back, we can navigate through these hurdles with greater clarity and resilience.

In this chapter, we'll delve deep into the most common impediments people face on their path to finding purpose. From societal pressures that mold our aspirations to internal barriers like fear and self-doubt, these challenges, though formidable, are not insurmountable.

By identifying and confronting them head-on, we can move closer to a life led by purpose and intention, rather than one dictated by external influences or internal apprehensions.

Societal Pressures and Misconceptions

In an era characterized by amplified communication through social media and an increasingly globalized world, societal pressures have evolved into a pervasive element of many individuals' lives. Societal pressures, in essence, refer to the expectations and norms that cultures, communities, and peer groups place upon individuals.

These pressures dictate how one should look, behave, achieve, and even feel, and they often define success by specific parameters like attaining a high-paying job, securing property, or having an "ideal" family structure.

A significant repercussion of these pressures is that they often overshadow one's personal desires, leading individuals to make life choices that may not resonate with their inner selves. For instance, many pursue careers based on what's deemed prestigious or lucrative rather than what aligns with their passion.

The fear of judgment, ostracization, or even just feeling left out pushes individuals towards choices they might not make otherwise. The narrative of achieving certain life milestones by a particular age—such as marriage, children, or promotions—also looms large, making many feel inadequate if their life trajectory doesn't match the "timeline."

Misconceptions play a crucial role in amplifying these societal pressures. Stereotypes, often perpetuated by media, dictate what's "normal" or "ideal." These misconceptions can manifest in various ways.

For instance, the belief that a person's worth is tied to their financial success, or that happiness comes from external accomplishments rather than internal fulfilment. The idea that certain professions are inherently superior to others, or that one's life path should be linear, are further misconceptions that people grapple with.

Another profound misconception is the portrayal of a "perfect" life on social media platforms. With curated images and stories of success, there's a perpetuated belief that everyone else has their life perfectly figured out, exacerbating feelings of inadequacy and alienation in others. This skewed portrayal creates a distorted reality where everyone strives for a perfection that doesn't exist, perpetually feeling unfulfilled in the process.

In navigating the maze of societal pressures and misconceptions, it's crucial for individuals to cultivate self-awareness, critical thinking, and genuine self-acceptance.

By recognizing and challenging these external forces, individuals can carve out paths that align more authentically with their true selves, rather than trying to fit into prefabricated molds.

Fear of Failure or Judgment

The fear of failure, often termed as "atychiphobia," is one of the most paralyzing emotions an individual can experience. Rooted deep within our psyche, it's a primal response that originates from our evolutionary desire to avoid danger.

In modern times, this fear isn't just about physical harm; it's about the emotional and psychological impact of not succeeding. For many, the mere thought of not meeting personal or societal standards—of attempting something and not succeeding—becomes an insurmountable obstacle.

This trepidation manifests in various ways: procrastination, a lack of self-confidence, or even a complete withdrawal from pursuing our goals and aspirations.

Parallel to the fear of failure is the fear of judgment. Living in interconnected communities means that we are constantly observed and assessed by those around us, and the modern world, with its social media platforms and constant connectivity, has only intensified this scrutiny.

This fear of being judged or criticized can be just as crippling as the fear of failure. It's a reflection of our intrinsic need for social acceptance, a vestige from times when being ostracized from a group could mean certain death.

Today, the stakes might not be as high, but the emotional toll can be significant. Being overly concerned about others' opinions can inhibit genuine self-expression, leading individuals to lead lives that align more with societal expectations than their authentic selves.

Both fears, of failure and judgment, are intertwined in a dance of self-doubt. They feed into each other, creating a feedback loop that can deter even the most passionate individuals from chasing their dreams.

While the fear of failure makes us question our abilities, the fear of judgment makes us question our worth in the eyes of others. Overcoming these fears requires introspection, resilience, and a conscious shift in perspective.

It means recognizing that failure is an intrinsic part of growth and that true fulfilment comes from authentic self-expression, not societal validation.

Lack of Self-awareness

Self-awareness, often heralded as one of the cornerstones of personal growth, refers to the conscious knowledge of one's own character, emotions, desires, strengths, and weaknesses.

When individuals possess self-awareness, they are better equipped to navigate complex social dynamics, manage their emotions, and lead a life in alignment with their values and aspirations.

Conversely, a lack of self-awareness can present multifaceted challenges in both personal and professional spheres.

At its core, a lack of self-awareness means being out of touch with one's inner world. This disconnection can manifest in various ways. Individuals may misinterpret their feelings, misunderstand their motivations, or remain blind to their behavioral patterns.

For example, someone might consistently feel agitated in crowded spaces but, without self-awareness, might never recognize their discomfort as stemming from a mild form of claustrophobia.

Instead, they might externalize the blame, perhaps believing others are acting provocatively or that certain places are inherently unpleasant.

Professionally, a lack of self-awareness can be especially detrimental. In the workplace, individuals who are not self-aware might repeatedly make the same mistakes, fail to recognize how their actions impact colleagues, or remain ignorant to the areas where they need improvement.

This not only hampers their personal growth but can also create discord in teams, lead to miscommunications, and contribute to a toxic work environment.

Moreover, relationships can be strained when one lacks self-awareness. Such individuals might struggle to understand the origins of their emotions, leading to misplaced anger, unjust blame, or an inability to communicate their feelings effectively.

For instance, someone might become irritated with their partner for not spending enough time with them, not realizing that their own insecurities or past experiences of abandonment are amplifying their emotional reactions.

Additionally, without self-awareness, personal growth and self-improvement become challenging pursuits. After all, to change or improve oneself, one must first recognize the areas that need attention.

This blind spot can lead individuals to chase goals that don't genuinely resonate with them, or worse, they might end up molding themselves based on societal expectations rather than their authentic desires.

In essence, while self-awareness is a journey and not necessarily a destination, the pitfalls of lacking it are profound.

It underscores the importance of introspection, seeking feedback, and being open to self-discovery, all of which are foundational to leading a fulfilling and authentic life.

Overemphasis on Material Success

In contemporary society, material success often acts as a yardstick for personal worth and achievement. The surge of consumerism, propelled by mass media and the rapid pace of technological advancements, has entrenched the belief that one's value can be gauged by tangible assets, from luxury cars and grand homes to brand-name clothing and the latest gadgets.

This yardstick, while prominently displayed in mainstream culture, often offers an oversimplified and skewed perspective on what constitutes a meaningful and fulfilled life.

The overemphasis on material success carries with it several consequences. For one, it can lead to a relentless chase for more, where an individual's aspirations become a never-ending ladder of acquiring the next big thing.

This "hedonic treadmill" can result in individuals feeling perpetually unsatisfied, as the elation from a new purchase or achievement tends to be temporary. Once the novelty wears off, the desire for something bigger or better takes its place.

Furthermore, equating material wealth with success can overshadow other equally valuable forms of success, such as building meaningful relationships, cultivating personal growth, contributing to the community, or even pursuing one's passions and creativity.

It reduces the multifaceted nature of human achievement and contentment to a singular dimension, often side-lining the intangible aspects of life that frequently provide deeper and more lasting satisfaction.

Another troubling aspect of this overemphasis is the pressure and stress it places on individuals, especially the younger generation. The desire to "keep up with the Joneses" can lead to overwork, mounting debt, and even unethical behavior as individuals strive to match or surpass the material successes flaunted by peers, celebrities, or influencers.

Moreover, when material success becomes the pinnacle of achievement, it often breeds an environment of comparison rather than collaboration. Instead of communities coming together to uplift one another, the focus shifts to outdoing one another, leading to divisions and feelings of inadequacy or superiority based on material possession.

In conclusion, while there's nothing inherently wrong with seeking material comfort or being proud of one's financial achievements, the problem arises when material success is seen as the primary or sole indicator of a life well-lived. True contentment and purpose often lie in a balance of material, emotional, relational, and spiritual fulfilment. It's essential for society to recognize and celebrate the diverse paths to success and fulfilment to foster a more holistic, inclusive, and contented world.

Chapter 5: Introspection - The First Step to Uncovering Purpose

In our relentless pursuit of external achievements, we often forget to turn inwards. We're inundated with stories of success, milestones reached, and accolades achieved.

However, when we pause and reflect, we realize that the loudest celebrations often come from accomplishments rooted deep within us—those aligned with our core beliefs, values, and purpose. This alignment isn't a happy accident but a result of sincere introspection.

Introspection, in essence, is the act of examining one's own conscious thoughts and feelings. It is not mere daydreaming, but an intentional act of diving deep into the recesses of our psyche to understand our motivations, desires, fears, and aspirations.

Why is this internal examination so crucial? Because within these depths lies the roadmap to our life's purpose. Every experience, emotion, and thought we've ever had contained hints about what truly resonates with us. Deciphering these hints requires not just a glance but a studied gaze inward.

In this chapter, we'll explore the art and science of introspection, understanding why it's the cornerstone of discovering one's life purpose.

Through exercises, anecdotes, and reflective practices, we'll embark on the transformative journey of understanding ourselves, setting the stage for the profound revelations that lie ahead.

The Importance of Self-Reflection

In the breakneck speed of our modern world, where notifications clamor for attention and a myriad of tasks pull us in every direction, pausing might seem like a luxury. But it is in these rare moments of quiet introspection that we discover the true essence of ourselves.

Self-reflection, the deliberate act of turning inward to examine thoughts, feelings, and motives, is a cornerstone of personal growth and self-awareness. It is an ancient practice, revered by philosophers and sages, yet in today's digital age, it holds even more significance.

Every individual embarks on a personal journey, one laden with challenges, achievements, failures, and aspirations. But how often do we stop to ask ourselves the meaning behind our actions, the reasons for our feelings, or the deeper motive driving our pursuits?

Without self-reflection, life can become a series of reactions, leaving us feeling lost in the grand tapestry of existence.

By dedicating time to self-reflection, we create a sacred space, a haven where we can confront our deepest fears, celebrate our successes, and understand our failures.

It allows us to cultivate mindfulness, align our actions with our values, and recognize patterns that may be hindering our progress. Ultimately, self-reflection offers us the clarity needed to navigate the complex voyage of life with intention and purpose.

As we delve into the subsequent chapters, we'll explore the intricacies of self-reflection, its myriad benefits, and the ways in which it can profoundly transform our lives.

Whether you're a seasoned introspector or just beginning your journey into the inner realms of your mind, this exploration promises to shed light on the untapped potential that lies within us all.

Introspection: Journaling Prompts, Meditation Practices, and Deep Questioning

In the vast, swirling cosmos of our minds, there exists a realm of thoughts, emotions, and memories that often go unexplored. In our fast-paced lives, we become so enmeshed in our daily routines and external engagements that the inner voice, our most authentic self, becomes a faint echo.

It's here, in this inner sanctum, that introspection becomes a beacon. By delving deep into our psyche, introspection not only allows us to better understand ourselves but also empowers us to mold a life that resonates with our true essence.

Among the most profound tools for introspection are journaling prompts, meditation practices, and deep questioning. Each of these techniques offers a unique pathway to our inner worlds.

Journaling, for instance, is akin to having an intimate conversation with oneself, capturing fleeting thoughts and emotions, crystallizing them onto paper.

Meditation, on the other hand, serves as a serene boat ride on the river of consciousness, allowing us to witness the ebb and flow of our thoughts without judgment.

And then there's deep questioning, a method of challenging our deeply held beliefs and assumptions, tearing down the walls of our mental constructs to reveal the vast landscapes of possibility.

In the chapters that follow, we'll embark on a journey of self-discovery using these tools. Through carefully crafted journaling prompts, we'll pen down our most profound reflections.

Guided meditation sessions will provide us with moments of clarity and peace. And a series of thought-provoking questions will challenge us to reconsider our worldviews and the essence of our being.

As you delve into these exercises, remember that introspection is not a destination but a continuous journey. It's not about finding the 'right' answers but about asking the right questions. And in this quest, every insight, every realization, no matter how small, is a step closer to the most authentic version of oneself.

Journaling Prompts:

Journaling is a self-reflective practice that allows individuals to explore their thoughts, feelings, and experiences on paper. It provides a safe space to confront one's innermost thoughts without judgment, thereby fostering self-awareness. Some effective journaling prompts to aid introspection include:

"What moments in my life have brought me the most joy, and why?"

"If I had all the resources and time in the world, what would I dedicate my life to?"

"What are three challenges I've overcome, and what did they teach me about myself?"

"Describe a time when I felt most alive."

"What values are non-negotiable in my life?"

"In what situations do I feel most authentic and true to myself?"

Approaching these prompts with an open mind and writing without censorship can lead to profound discoveries about one's aspirations, fears, values, and more.

Meditation Practices:

Meditation is another profound method of introspection. Unlike journaling, which uses words and thoughts to navigate one's inner world, meditation allows us to explore our consciousness without the constant chatter of the mind. Some meditation practices for introspection include:

Mindfulness Meditation: This involves being present and fully engaged with the here and now. By focusing on our breath or other bodily sensations, we learn to observe our thoughts without judgment, thereby gaining insights into our patterns of thinking.

Guided Visualization: Here, guided audio or an instructor leads you through a series of visual scenarios, often designed to unlock deeper feelings or aspirations. For instance, visualizing a safe haven can reveal what environments or situations you find most comforting and why.

Loving-kindness Meditation: This practice involves sending out feelings of love and kindness first to oneself and then to others. It can unveil deeply held feelings of self-worth, forgiveness, and compassion.

Deep Questioning:

Deep questioning involves engaging in profound, thought-provoking questions that challenge existing beliefs and encourage inner exploration. Unlike casual questions, deep questions aim to reach the core of one's beliefs, motivations, and desires. Examples of deep questions include:

"What does success mean to me, and why?"

"If fear was not a factor, what would I do differently in my life?"

"What are the stories I tell myself that might be holding me back?"

"How do my daily actions align with my long-term goals and values?"

Engaging in deep questioning, either through self-reflection, discussions with trusted individuals, or guided therapy, can unveil underlying motivations, unexplored dreams, and hidden reservations. The key is to approach these questions with curiosity rather than judgment, allowing for a genuine exploration of one's psyche.

Incorporating these introspective exercises into one's routine can be transformative. Whether through the written word, meditative practices, or probing inquiries, the journey inward can lead to a clearer understanding of one's purpose, motivations, and authentic self.

Chapter 6: Exploring Passions and Strengths

In the maze of life, amidst its many twists and turns, passions and strengths serve as our guiding stars. They are the raw materials from which our life's purpose is often forged.

Many of us mistakenly believe that discovering our purpose is about seeking something outside of ourselves, something grand or previously unattainable. Yet, more often than not, it lies dormant within us, waiting to be recognized, nurtured, and expressed.

Imagine passions as the flames that ignite our souls, the interests and pursuits that make our hearts race a little faster. They are often the activities that absorb us so completely that we lose track of time, the topics we could discuss for hours without tiring.

On the other hand, our strengths are the natural talents and abilities we possess, the tasks we excel at without much effort, the roles we naturally assume in group settings. When combined, our passions and strengths create a powerful synergy, leading us closer to our authentic purpose.

This chapter is designed to be a voyage of self-discovery. We'll delve deep into understanding our passions—not just fleeting interests but deep-rooted callings that resonate with our core.

We'll also journey into recognizing and harnessing our strengths, turning them into potent tools to serve our purpose. By the end of this chapter, you should have a clearer compass reading, pointing you toward the North Star of your life's true calling.

Activities to Identify and Evaluate Your Strengths

Uncovering and understanding your innate strengths is pivotal to both personal and professional growth. Recognizing what you naturally excel at can give you a clearer direction and drive in life, helping align your actions with your core competencies. Here are some activities to help you identify and evaluate your strengths:

Self-reflection and Journaling: Begin with introspection. Dedicate quiet moments to think about the tasks or actions that come easily to you or those activities that you enjoy the most.

Often, the things we enjoy are directly tied to our inherent strengths. Journaling these thoughts can provide clarity. Over time, by reading back through your entries, patterns may emerge that indicate particular strengths.

Feedback from Friends and Family: Sometimes, we're blind to our own strengths, or we undervalue them. Those close to us often see our abilities more clearly. Ask friends, family, or colleagues about the strengths they observe in you. You might be surprised by what they see that you've overlooked.

Take a Strengths Assessment Test: There are several renowned psychological assessments designed to pinpoint your strengths. You can find these strength assessment tests online.

These tests have been crafted and refined over years to provide accurate results, giving you a comprehensive understanding of your strengths.

Evaluate Past Successes: Think about your past achievements, both big and small. What were the common skills or qualities you employed to achieve those successes? Often, by analyzing our past achievements, we can deduce the strengths that enabled those victories.

Engage in New Activities: Sometimes, we discover our strengths when we push ourselves out of our comfort zones. Engaging in a new hobby, joining a workshop, or volunteering can expose you to different situations and tasks. Through these experiences, you might uncover strengths you didn't know you had.

Consult with a Career or Life Coach: These professionals are trained to help individuals identify their strengths and weaknesses. Through sessions with them, which often involve a mix of discussions, exercises, and assessments, you can get a clear picture of your inherent strengths.

Analyze Feedback and Criticism: While we often focus on the negative aspects of feedback or criticism, there's usually a silver lining. If you consistently receive positive feedback about a particular skill or trait, it's likely one of your strengths.

In conclusion, understanding your strengths is about merging self-awareness with external perspectives. It's a balance of introspective activities and seeking feedback from tests or trusted individuals.

By actively engaging in these activities, you not only discover your strengths but also learn how to leverage them effectively in various aspects of your life.

How to Differentiate Between Fleeting Passions and Genuine Callings

Passions and callings are both powerful driving forces in our lives. However, there's a fine line between the two, and it's important to recognize their distinctions to lead a life aligned with true purpose.

Fleeting Passions:

Passions can be thought of as intense, yet sometimes transient, interests or enthusiasms. They are often fueled by immediate fascination or a sudden surge of excitement.

These are the hobbies or interests we might pick up after being inspired by a movie, a conversation, or a short-lived personal experience. For instance, after watching a documentary on rock climbing, one might feel a strong urge to take it up, only to realize after a few sessions that the interest has waned.

Fleeting passions tend to be highly responsive to external stimuli, and while they're strong, they might not have deep roots. They can change based on the latest trends, societal influences, or immediate surroundings.

There's absolutely nothing wrong with having fleeting passions; they add variety and excitement to our lives. However, they might not provide a sustainable path or a deeper sense of fulfilment in the long run.

Genuine Callings:

On the other hand, genuine callings are deep-seated desires or vocations that align with our core values, skills, and life experiences.

They are consistent and persistent over time, often feeling like a magnetic pull toward a particular path or purpose.

Genuine callings go beyond short-lived enthusiasm; they resonate with our very identity and sense of self. They are the dreams or ambitions we keep coming back to, even after facing setbacks or diversions.

For instance, someone might feel a consistent drive to advocate for mental health because of personal experiences or a profound understanding of its societal importance.

This drive remains, regardless of external influences or changing circumstances. Callings often bring a deep sense of satisfaction, not just from the activity itself but from the alignment with one's inner values and beliefs.

Navigating the Difference:

To differentiate between fleeting passions and genuine callings, introspection is key. Regularly take stock of your interests. Ask yourself: Is this something I've been consistently drawn to over the years? Or is it a recent fascination?

Another helpful strategy is to assess the depth of your interest. A fleeting passion might involve a surface-level interest, while a genuine calling often encourages you to dive deeper, learn more, and engage at a profound level.

Furthermore, pay attention to how you feel when obstacles arise. While you might easily give up on a fleeting passion when faced with challenges, a genuine calling usually motivates you to push through, adapt, and persevere.

Chapter 7: Your Life's Experiences as Clues

Every individual's life is a unique tapestry woven from threads of experiences, challenges, victories, lessons, and emotions. While, at times, certain events might seem random or devoid of deeper significance, with closer introspection, they can provide illuminating insights into one's authentic self and purpose.

Think of your life as a novel. Every chapter, every page, and every paragraph contribute to the story's progression, often leaving behind subtle clues about the protagonist's true essence and destiny.

Similarly, your life's experiences, whether they're monumental milestones or seemingly inconsequential moments, can serve as pivotal indicators guiding you toward your life's purpose.

In this chapter, we'll delve deep into the art of reading and interpreting these clues. We'll offer exercises to help you map out your life's timeline, pinpointing and reflecting on those transformative events that have shaped you.

By the end, you'll see that finding your purpose is not always about looking externally for answers, but often about understanding and embracing your own life's narrative.

Mapping Your Life Timeline: Key Events and Their Significance

Mapping your life timeline is akin to laying out the chapters of your own autobiography. It's a process that allows you to visualize the significant events, turning points, highs, and lows that have shaped who you are today.

This journey through time can offer profound insights into patterns, decisions, and moments that have steered your life's course, often revealing underlying themes or passions that you might not have been consciously aware of.

Every person's life is punctuated by key events. These might include obvious milestones like graduating from school, landing your first job, or getting married.

But equally as significant are the subtler moments: the summer you discovered a love for painting, the time you stood up for a friend and recognized your own inner strength, or the evening you looked up at the stars and felt a deep connection to the universe.

These experiences, both grand and seemingly inconsequential, play pivotal roles in shaping our beliefs, values, and understanding of the world.

However, the mere act of noting down events isn't enough. Delving into their significance is where the real introspection begins.

For instance, why was traveling solo to a foreign country a key event in your life? Was it because you embraced independence, confronted your fears, or experienced a culture that drastically altered your perspectives? By understanding the 'why' behind each event, you begin to uncover the threads that weave the fabric of your being.

Furthermore, mapping your life's timeline isn't just about the past. It's a tool that can help project future aspirations and goals. Recognizing patterns in past events can guide decisions and pathways in the coming years. If helping a family member through a tough time was a pivotal moment for you, it might indicate a deep-seated desire to assist others, possibly pointing towards a career or volunteer work in counselling or caregiving.

In essence, mapping your life timeline is a self-reflective journey that provides a bird's-eye view of your life's trajectory. It's an exercise in understanding, accepting, and learning from the past while drawing inspiration and direction for the future.

The beauty of this exercise is its inherent personalization; no two timelines are the same, and each one tells a unique, evolving story of an individual's journey through life.

Exercises to Derive Meaning and Patterns from Past Experiences

1. Timeline Creation

Materials: Large piece of paper or poster board, markers or colored pens, stickers or post-its (optional).

Instructions:

1. Lay out the paper horizontally.
2. Mark your birth at the far-left end and the current year at the far-right end.
3. Begin plotting significant events chronologically from left to right. These can include accomplishments, challenges, milestones, pivotal decisions, etc.
4. For each event, write a brief description and the year it took place.
5. Use different colours or symbols to represent various types of events (e.g., red for challenges, green for accomplishments).

2. Event Deep Dive

Materials: A journal or notepad, a pen.

Instructions:

1. Choose one significant event from your timeline.
2. Reflect on the event and write answers to the following:

- What happened?
- How did I feel at the time?
- Why was this event significant to me?
- What did I learn from this experience?
- How has this event influenced or shaped my subsequent decisions or life path?

3. Connecting the Dots

Materials: Your life timeline, a journal or notepad, colored pens.

Instructions:

1. Review your timeline and identify any patterns or recurring themes. For example, did you notice a trend of taking risks, pursuing creative outlets, or advocating for others?
2. Write down these patterns.
3. Reflect on what these patterns might reveal about your passions, values, or strengths.

4. Future Projections

Materials: Your life timeline, sticky notes or paper, a pen.

Instructions:

1. Think about where you would like to see yourself in 5, 10, and 20 years.

2. On separate sticky notes, write down goals or milestones you'd like to achieve in those timeframes.
3. Place these notes on the extended portion of your timeline, beyond the current year.
4. Reflect on the steps or decisions you might need to take to reach these goals.

5. Photo Reflection

Materials: Old photographs, a journal or notepad, a pen.

Instructions:

1. Browse through old photographs from different phases of your life.
2. Choose a photo that evokes strong memories or emotions.
3. Write about the moment captured in the photo, its significance, and any memories it brings back.

6. Feedback Session

Materials: Your life timeline, a trusted friend or family member.

Instructions:

1. Share your life timeline with someone close to you.

2. Ask them to share their perspective on the events you've marked.

3. Note down any insights or perspectives they offer that you hadn't considered. Often, others might notice patterns or significant moments that we've overlooked.

These exercises aim to guide introspection, helping you gain clarity about your past, recognize patterns, and derive insights for future endeavors.

Chapter 8: Aligning Your Purpose with Greater Good

In our journey towards unearthing our life's purpose, it is easy to become ensnared in the trappings of personal gain or validation.

The allure of individual success, accolades, and materialistic achievements can often cloud the profound depth of what purpose truly encapsulates.

Yet, as history and countless narratives show us, the most fulfilling and resonant purposes often transcend the self. They intertwine seamlessly with the broader tapestry of humanity and seek to uplift, heal, connect, and transform.

Aligning one's purpose with the greater good does not merely imply grand gestures or monumental shifts. It is about recognizing that our highest calling often lies in serving others, in being a part of something larger than ourselves.

This alignment resonates deeply within us, offering not only personal satisfaction but also creating ripples of positive impact in the world around us.

In this chapter, we'll delve into the symbiotic relationship between personal purpose and the greater good.

Through poignant case studies, introspective exercises, and transformative insights, you'll discover how intertwining your purpose with the broader needs of the world can amplify its power, providing a deeper sense of fulfilment and creating lasting change.

How Serving Others Can Amplify Your Purpose

Finding one's purpose often goes beyond personal desires or achievements. At its core, a truly fulfilling purpose often intersects with the well-being of others. When we serve others, our sense of purpose is not only validated but also magnified in multiple dimensions.

Firstly, serving others creates a tangible impact. While personal goals can sometimes be intangible or abstract, the act of serving offers direct results, whether it's seeing a smile on someone's face, witnessing a community thrive, or helping someone overcome a hurdle.

This tangibility reinforces the belief that one's purpose holds genuine value in the broader context of society. When we witness the fruits of our actions and their effect on others, it provides a feedback loop that reinforces our sense of purpose and its meaningfulness.

Moreover, serving others often leads to deeper connections and relationships. Humans are inherently social beings. When we aid, guide, or uplift someone, it fosters a bond based on gratitude, mutual respect, and shared experiences. These connections serve as a reminder that our purpose is not an isolated quest; instead, it's intricately linked with the lives and stories of others. Through these connections, we often find validation, support, and further clarity in our purposeful journey.

Additionally, serving others can broaden our perspectives. Engaging with diverse individuals and communities exposes us to varied life stories, challenges, and aspirations.

By understanding the multifaceted tapestry of human experiences, we can refine and expand our purpose. For instance, someone who finds purpose in teaching might discover, through service, that they are not just imparting knowledge but also empowering individuals, fostering community growth, or even bridging cultural divides. This expanded perspective can amplify the depth and reach of one's purpose.

Lastly, there's a profound psychological and emotional enrichment that comes from serving others. Numerous studies have shown that altruistic actions, from volunteering to simple acts of kindness, boost our mental well-being. This sense of fulfilment and happiness, derived from the act of giving, can act as fuel, driving us further in our purpose-driven endeavors. In a way, it's a symbiotic relationship; our purpose guides us to serve, and the act of service, in turn, enriches and amplifies our purpose.

While personal reflection and introspection are critical to discovering one's purpose, the act of serving others acts as a catalyst, taking our understanding of purpose from a theoretical concept to a lived experience. Through service, our purpose finds validation, depth, and, most importantly, a heartfelt connection to the world around us.

Case Studies of Individuals Whose Purposes Align with Larger Causes

In a world brimming with individual pursuits, there exists a unique breed of individuals whose aspirations synchronize harmoniously with larger, more universal causes.

These individuals do not just chase personal dreams but intertwine their ambitions with goals that resonate on a broader spectrum, transcending borders, cultures, and communities. Their stories are not just their own; they become tales of hope, inspiration, and impact for society at large.

These case studies delve into the lives of such remarkable individuals. Through their narratives, we uncover how personal revelations can burgeon into movements, how one's purpose can amplify to echo and serve the needs of many, and how the magic truly unfolds when personal passion meets a universal problem.

Whether it was a single event that acted as a catalyst, a lifelong observation of a pervasive issue, or an inherent, inexplicable drive to serve, each story in this collection will provide a testament to the power of aligning personal purpose with greater good.

In these pages, you won't just find tales of success; you'll discover journeys fraught with challenges, introspections, failures, and resolute determinations.

As you embark on this exploration, may you be inspired by the limitless possibilities that emerge when personal purpose is wielded as a tool for broader change.

May these stories remind you that while individual aspirations are potent, when they align with larger causes, they become transformative forces that shape societies, touch lives, and build legacies.

Nelson Mandela: A Lifelong Fight for Equality and Justice

Nelson Mandela's name is synonymous with the anti-apartheid movement in South Africa. Facing racial prejudice first-hand, Mandela's larger purpose became evident as he dedicated his life to establishing equal rights for all South Africans, regardless of their race.

He endured 27 years in prison, facing inhumane conditions and isolation, but his spirit remained unbroken. Upon his release, instead of seeking vengeance, Mandela championed reconciliation between the country's racial groups.

As South Africa's first black president, his leadership was emblematic of his commitment to justice, equality, and nation-building. Mandela's life serves as a testament to the idea that individual purpose, when aligned with universal values of justice and equality, can usher in transformative societal change.

Mother Teresa: Serving the Poorest of the Poor

Mother Teresa's humble journey began as a nun, but her encounters with the destitute and dying on the streets of Kolkata, India, defined her life's larger purpose. Guided by compassion and a profound love for humanity, she established the Missionaries of Charity, an order dedicated to serving the "poorest of the poor".

Whether it was lepers, orphans, or the dying, Mother Teresa and her sisters provided care and love, emphasizing the inherent dignity of every individual. Her life's work, rooted in selfless service, highlighted the global issue of extreme poverty and the moral imperative to address it.

Even posthumously, her mission continues to inspire countless individuals and organizations worldwide to serve those marginalized and forgotten by society.

Malala Yousafzai: An Advocate for Girls' Education

Malala Yousafzai's life took a dramatic turn when, as a teenager, she was shot by the Taliban for advocating for girls' education in Pakistan. However, the near-fatal incident only strengthened her resolve.

Malala's purpose transcended beyond her personal experiences as she became a global advocate for female education. Recognizing the systemic barriers and threats girls faced in many parts of the world in accessing education, Malala, along with her father, co-founded the Malala Fund.

This organization seeks to ensure 12 years of free, safe, and quality education for every girl. Her relentless advocacy and poignant articulation of the cause earned her the Nobel Peace Prize in 2014, making her the youngest-ever Nobel laureate.

Elon Musk: A Vision for a Sustainable Future

When one thinks of entrepreneurs with a larger-than-life vision that aligns with global needs, Elon Musk often comes to mind. Musk's ventures, from Tesla to SpaceX to SolarCity, all seem disparate at a glance.

However, they cohesively point towards a singular purpose: ensuring the long-term survival and betterment of humanity. With Tesla, Musk aims to combat climate change by pushing the transition to electric vehicles and sustainable energy.

SpaceX, on the other hand, has the overarching mission of making humans a multi-planetary species, with Mars colonization as a potential safeguard against earthly catastrophes. Musk's ventures, driven by this broader purpose, have spurred innovations and shifted industries towards more sustainable practices, all while aligning with the cause of safeguarding humanity's future.

Jane Goodall: Pioneering Conservation and Animal Rights

From a young age, Jane Goodall exhibited a profound love for animals and nature. This passion led her to the Gombe Stream National Park in Tanzania, where she conducted her ground-breaking research on wild chimpanzees.

Instead of merely studying these animals, Goodall recognized the intrinsic value of their lives and their significance to the broader ecosystem. Her findings revolutionized our understanding of primates and challenged traditional notions of what distinguishes humans from animals.

Over the years, Goodall's purpose expanded to include global environmental conservation and activism against animal cruelty. The Jane Goodall Institute, founded by her, works towards wildlife research, education, and conservation.

As a UN Messenger of Peace and through various initiatives, Goodall has consistently advocated for understanding and conserving the natural world, highlighting the interconnectedness of all living beings.

Paul Farmer: Bridging Healthcare Gaps in Impoverished Regions As a physician and anthropologist, Dr. Paul Farmer recognized the gross inequities in healthcare access and quality, particularly in resource-poor settings.

Determined to address this, he co-founded Partners in Health (PIH) in 1987. PIH's mission was to bring the benefits of modern medical science to those most in need and to serve as an antidote to despair. Through his work in Haiti and other underserved regions,

Farmer's larger purpose emerged: to transform global health and challenge the status quo that accepted vast disparities in care. His endeavors have been instrumental in redefining healthcare as a fundamental human right and establishing new standards for care in impoverished areas.

Wangari Maathai: Planting Trees, Cultivating Hope

In Kenya, Wangari Maathai saw how deforestation and environmental degradation adversely affected local communities, especially women.

It impacted their access to clean water, firewood, and fertile soil. In response, she founded the Green Belt Movement in 1977, an environmental organization that promotes the planting of trees to restore environments and empower communities.

But Maathai's vision went beyond reforestation. Her purpose aligned with larger causes like women's rights, community empowerment, and environmental conservation. Despite facing personal risks, including imprisonment, Maathai's efforts led to the planting of over 50 million trees and inspired a global tree-planting movement. In 2004, she became the first African woman to receive the Nobel Peace Prize, acknowledging her contribution to "sustainable development, democracy, and peace."

Kailash Satyarthi: Rescuing the Stolen Childhoods

Witnessing child labor in his home country of India, Kailash Satyarthi was moved by the plight of these children, robbed of their childhood and basic rights. Founding the 'Bachpan Bachao Andolan' (Save the Childhood Movement), Satyarthi's purpose became inextricably linked with the larger cause of child rights and the abolition of child labor.

Through grassroots activism, legal interventions, and direct actions, Satyarthi and his team have rescued thousands of children from forced labor, providing them with rehabilitation and education.

His tireless efforts culminated in the Nobel Peace Prize in 2014, which he shared with Malala Yousafzai, acknowledging their combined struggle against the suppression of children.

Temple Grandin: Advocating for Autism and Animal Welfare

Born with autism, Temple Grandin's unique perspective allowed her to form a special connection and understanding of animals. As she grew older, her deep empathy for animals, particularly livestock, led her to advocate for their humane treatment.

Not only did she design innovative systems for handling livestock with care and compassion, but she also became a vocal advocate for animal rights. Simultaneously, Grandin's own experiences with autism made her a spokesperson for neurodiversity, educating the world on the potential and capabilities of those with different cognitive perspectives.

Through her dual advocacy, Grandin's purpose converged with broader causes, championing both animal welfare and the recognition and inclusion of neurodivergent individuals.

Viktor Frankl: Finding Meaning Amidst Adversity

As a neurologist, psychiatrist, and Holocaust survivor, Viktor Frankl's experiences in Nazi concentration camps deeply influenced his life's work.

Emerging from the horrors of the Holocaust, he penned "Man's Search for Meaning," where he posited that even in the face of profound suffering, humans could find purpose and meaning. Frankl founded logotherapy, a form of existential analysis that emphasizes the human search for meaning.

His personal trials and subsequent academic work aligned with the larger cause of mental health and well-being, offering countless individual's tools to navigate life's challenges and find purpose.

Chapter 9: Tools and Resources to Help Find Your Purpose

Embarking on the journey to discover your life's purpose can often feel like navigating a vast, unfamiliar wilderness. While introspection and self-awareness are our internal compasses, they sometimes need calibration.

Just as an explorer might require maps, guides, or even stars to steer them in the right direction, those seeking their purpose can benefit from tools and resources designed to illuminate the path ahead.

In the digital age, where information is abundant and the world's collective wisdom is at our fingertips, a plethora of tools and resources awaits eager souls yearning for meaning.

These instruments don't offer direct answers—no book, workshop, or mentor can tell you outright what your life's purpose is. Instead, they act as catalysts, prompting questions, fostering insights, and providing frameworks that aid in your self-discovery journey.

This chapter is a curated guide, a treasury if you will, of some of the most transformative tools and resources that have empowered thousands to hone in on their true calling.

From age-old books that resonate with timeless wisdom to modern digital platforms fostering communities of seekers, we will delve deep into the tools you can harness in your quest.

Prepare to explore, question, and engage. These tools and resources are your allies, waiting to be tapped into, as you unfold the chapters of your life's most profound quest.

Books, workshops, seminars, and retreats

In the quest for self-improvement and personal growth, individuals often seek external resources to guide, inspire, and facilitate their journey. Books, workshops, seminars, and retreats represent the four pillars of experiential and intellectual learning.

Each offers a unique avenue to self-discovery and enlightenment, catering to diverse learning styles and preferences.

Books

Books have long been the cornerstone of self-improvement and the search for purpose. They offer timeless wisdom, providing insights into personal experiences and academic research.

- Depth and Breadth: Books can delve deeply into a topic, offering comprehensive information that is often hard to find in shorter formats. This depth allows readers to immerse themselves and often revisit content for clarity.

  Example: Man's Search for Meaning by Viktor E. Frankl delves deep into the psychology of purpose through personal experiences and observations.

- Accessibility: One of the main benefits of books is their accessibility. They can be read at one's own pace, anywhere, and anytime. This flexibility allows individuals to integrate learning seamlessly into their lives.

E-books, audiobooks, and traditional print cater to various reading preferences.

- Diversity of Perspectives: The vast array of books available offers readers a chance to explore multiple viewpoints and experiences, helping to shape and refine their understanding of purpose.

From autobiographies to self-help and academic research, the choices are vast.

Workshops

Workshops are interactive sessions designed to teach or enhance specific skills or knowledge. They are often hands-on, allowing participants to engage actively with the material.

- Practical Learning: Unlike passive methods of learning, workshops are experiential. Participants not only receive information but also apply it in real-time.

Role-playing, group discussions, and practical exercises are common components.

- Expert Guidance: Workshops are typically facilitated by experts who can provide guidance, answer questions, and offer personalized feedback.

The direct interaction with facilitators can provide clarity and direction.

- Networking Opportunities: Attending workshops allows participants to connect with like-minded individuals, fostering community, and support.

These connections can lead to further learning opportunities and collaborations.

Seminars

Seminars are formal presentations or lectures on specific topics. They are generally more academic and informative than workshops but can still be interactive.

- Knowledge Transfer: Seminars are excellent for imparting large amounts of information in a structured manner.

Presenters often use multimedia, such as slides or videos, to enhance understanding.

- Q&A Sessions: Most seminars incorporate a question-and-answer segment, allowing attendees to clarify doubts and delve deeper into specific areas of interest.

This interaction bridges the gap between passive learning and active engagement.

- Exposure to Thought Leaders: Seminars often feature experts or thought leaders in a particular field, providing attendees with insights based on years of research or experience.

    Listening to various speakers offers a well-rounded perspective on the topic at hand.

Retreats

Retreats are immersive experiences, often spanning several days, designed to provide participants with a break from their routine and immerse them in a specific subject or practice.

- Intensive Learning: Given their extended nature, retreats offer a deep dive into topics. This format can be particularly beneficial for transformative subjects like finding one's purpose.

    Daily schedules often combine lectures, workshops, and personal reflection time.

- Change of Environment: By being in a new or secluded setting, participants can break free from daily distractions, enabling deeper introspection.

Natural settings, like mountain retreats or beachside venues, can enhance the experience.

- Holistic Approach: Many retreats incorporate holistic practices, such as yoga or meditation, to complement the learning process.

This combination of mental, emotional, and physical activities fosters personal growth.

Role of Mentors and Coaches

Mentors and coaches play pivotal roles in personal and professional development. Their influence can be the turning point for individuals navigating challenges, seeking growth, or aspiring to attain specific goals. While both roles offer guidance and support, they do so in distinct ways and under different dynamics.

Mentors:

- Long-Term Relationships:

Mentoring often involves building long-term relationships. These connections might last for years, offering evolving guidance as the mentee progresses through different stages of life or career.

- Experience-Based Guidance:

Mentors provide insights based on their own experiences. They've "been there and done that," offering a roadmap and highlighting potential pitfalls.

This first-hand knowledge is invaluable for mentees, helping them avoid common mistakes and take calculated risks.

- Holistic Support:

Beyond just career or skill development, mentors often provide holistic guidance, touching on personal growth, values, and broader life decisions.

- Networking:

Mentors often introduce mentees to their professional or personal networks, opening doors to opportunities, collaborations, or partnerships.

- Empowerment:

A mentor's belief in the mentee's potential can be a powerful motivator. This trust and support can empower mentees to take bold steps and believe in their capabilities.

Coaches:

- Structured Approach:

Coaching is typically more structured than mentoring. Coaches often employ specific methodologies, tools, and strategies to help individuals achieve their goals.

- Short-Term or Goal-Oriented:

Coaching engagements can be short-term or focused on particular objectives. Whether it's enhancing a skill, overcoming a challenge, or transitioning to a new role, coaches provide targeted support.

- Feedback and Accountability:

Coaches provide regular feedback, allowing individuals to understand their areas of strength and those needing improvement.

They also hold their clients accountable, ensuring that they're making progress and staying committed to their goals.

- Skill Development:

Coaches often specialize in specific areas, such as leadership coaching, life coaching, or skills coaching. This specialization allows them to offer expert guidance tailored to individual needs.

- Neutral Perspective:

Unlike mentors, who might share personal experiences, coaches often maintain a neutral stance, helping individuals find their solutions and path.

In summary, both mentors and coaches are integral to personal and professional development. While mentors offer the wisdom of experience and a broader, relationship-based support system, coaches provide focused, structured guidance to help individuals achieve specific goals or navigate particular challenges. The choice between seeking a mentor or coach—or even both—depends on the individual's needs, goals, and current life stage.

Chapter 10: Overcoming Challenges and Staying the Course

Discovering one's life purpose is an illuminating journey, but like all quests of significance, it's interspersed with hurdles and challenges. Some of these obstacles are external, manifesting as societal pressures or criticisms from those around us.

Others lurk within our minds, often taking the form of self-doubt, fear, or a wavering commitment when the path gets rocky. But just as a ship needs to weather storms to reach its destination, we too must face these challenges head-on to fully embrace and live out our purpose.

In this chapter, we will delve deep into the most common challenges people face when trying to align their lives with their purpose. More importantly, we'll equip you with practical strategies and insights to navigate these challenges.

Because finding your purpose is not a one-time event; it's a continuous journey. And to remain steadfast on this path, you need to be resilient, adaptable, and deeply committed, even when the going gets tough.

Join us as we explore not just how to overcome obstacles, but how to use them as stepping stones, making you stronger, more resilient, and more connected to your purpose with each challenge you surmount.

Handling Doubts and Criticisms

In the pursuit of any meaningful endeavor, it's inevitable to encounter doubts and criticisms. These uncertainties can stem from our internal fears or from external sources like friends, family, or even strangers.

Handling them gracefully and constructively can make a significant difference in our journey towards achieving our goals and finding our life's purpose.

Internal Doubts

Self-awareness: Recognizing and acknowledging your doubts is the first step. It's natural to question ourselves, especially when we're charting unfamiliar territory.

- Keep a journal to record moments of doubt, allowing you to reflect and address each concern systematically.
- Understand that everyone, even the most successful individuals, experiences self-doubt at various points in their lives.

Affirmations and Positive Self-talk: Our internal dialogue significantly impacts our mindset.

- Create a list of positive affirmations tailored to your goals and purpose.
- Remind yourself of past achievements and how you overcame previous doubts.

Seek Mentorship: Having a mentor or a coach can provide guidance, especially when you're lost or uncertain.

- They offer a different perspective, often based on more experience.
- Regular sessions can help you navigate personal doubts and provide actionable solutions.

External Criticisms

Constructive vs. Destructive Criticism: It's essential to distinguish between feedback that's genuinely helpful and criticism that's meant to demoralize.

- Constructive criticism can help you improve and refine your approach.
- Destructive criticism often says more about the critic than about your work or purpose.

Establish Boundaries: While it's important to be open to feedback, it's equally vital to set boundaries.

- Politely but firmly let people know when their unsolicited advice isn't welcome.
- Limit exposure to consistently negative or unsupportive individuals.

Reflect and Respond: Instead of reacting immediately, take time to reflect upon the criticism received.

- Consider if there's any truth or actionable advice in the feedback.
- If addressing the criticism, respond calmly and rationally, avoiding emotional confrontations.

Reaffirm Your Purpose: When faced with overwhelming criticism, return to the root of your purpose.

- Remind yourself why you started this journey.
- Visualize the positive impact of achieving your goals, using it as motivation to push past the noise of naysayers.

In the end, doubts and criticisms are par for the course when pursuing one's life purpose. However, with the right strategies and a resilient mindset, they can be transformed into tools for growth and clarity.

Surrounding Yourself with Supportive Communities

The old adage, "You are the average of the five people you spend the most time with," attributed to motivational speaker Jim Rohn, captures the essence of why surrounding oneself with a supportive community is pivotal.

In the journey of life, especially when venturing into new territories or pursuing grand visions, the significance of being encircled by a nurturing community cannot be overstated.

Benefits of a Supportive Community:

- ❖ Mental and Emotional Well-being:
  - A supportive community offers a safety net during challenging times.
  - Sharing concerns and victories with people who understand magnifies joy and divides sorrow, thereby acting as a therapeutic channel.
- ❖ Resource Pooling:
  - Members often bring diverse skills, experiences, and perspectives.
  - Collaboration within communities can lead to better problem-solving and resource sharing, from tangible assets to invaluable advice.
- ❖ Accountability:

- When you share your goals and aspirations with a community, they often hold you accountable.
- This form of accountability can act as a motivational force, pushing individuals to achieve their objectives and stay true to their commitments.

❖ Networking:

- Being part of a community naturally expands one's network.
- This expanded network can open doors to opportunities, partnerships, and collaborations that might have been otherwise inaccessible.

❖ Learning and Growth:

- Communities often foster an environment of continuous learning.
- By interacting with others, sharing experiences, and sometimes even formal training or workshops, members benefit from collective knowledge.

Finding the Right Community:

While the benefits of being in a supportive community are manifold, it's crucial to ensure that one aligns with the right kind of group. Here are some tips:

❖ Shared Vision and Values:

- Look for communities that resonate with your personal or professional values and aspirations.
- A shared vision can act as a binding force, ensuring long-term cohesion and mutual support.

❖ Diversity:

- Opt for communities that value diversity in thought, background, and expertise.
- Diverse groups bring a richness of perspective, enhancing the depth of discussions and collaborations.

❖ Openness and Respect:

- The foundation of any supportive community is mutual respect.
- Ensure that members are open to different viewpoints and that there's a culture of respect and empathy.

❖ Opportunities for Active Participation:

- Engage in communities where you can actively contribute, rather than just being a passive member.
- Active participation not only adds value to the group but also enriches one's personal experience.

In the digital age, communities are not restricted by geographical boundaries. From online forums, social media groups to local clubs, workshops, and meet-ups, the avenues to find and engage with like-minded individuals are abundant. The key lies in recognizing the immense value these communities bring and investing time and effort in nurturing these relationships.

Continual learning and re-evaluation

Continual Learning

Continual Learning is a sustained process of acquiring new knowledge, skills, and understanding throughout an individual's lifetime. In our rapidly evolving world, staying updated and learning continuously is no longer a luxury but a necessity. Here's why:

- ❖ Adapting to Change: With industries and technologies evolving at an unprecedented rate, continual learning ensures that individuals can adapt and stay relevant.
  - Professionals can keep up with the latest developments in their field.
  - Individuals can pivot their careers based on emerging opportunities or trends.
- ❖ Personal Growth: Beyond professional benefits, continuous learning contributes to personal enrichment.
  - New learning can introduce fresh perspectives or hobbies.
  - It keeps the mind active, potentially delaying cognitive decline in older age.
- ❖ Building Confidence: As one acquires new skills and knowledge, it can boost self-esteem and confidence.
  - Each new thing learned adds a feather to one's cap, expanding horizons and competence.

❖ Problem Solving: Continuous learning equips individuals with a broader set of tools to tackle challenges.

- Exposure to diverse subjects can stimulate creative solutions.
- It can promote a growth mindset, where challenges are viewed as opportunities to learn.

Re-evaluation

Re-evaluation is the periodic introspection and reflection on one's path, goals, and strategies. As individuals grow and contexts change, re-evaluation ensures alignment with one's evolving aspirations and the external environment.

❖ Alignment with Goals: Over time, personal or professional goals might shift. Regularly re-evaluating ensures that one's actions align with these changes.

- For instance, a professional might realize they value work-life balance over rapid career progression.
- Personal aspirations, like starting a family or pursuing a hobby, can shift focus.

❖ Optimizing Strategies: Even if goals remain consistent, the strategies to achieve them might need revision.

- New information or experiences can introduce better ways to reach objectives.

- Periodic assessment can highlight redundant efforts or resource drains.
- ❖ Emotional and Mental Well-being: Taking the time to introspect can be therapeutic.
  - Recognizing and addressing sources of dissatisfaction or burnout.
  - Celebrating achieved milestones and setting sights on new ones.
- ❖ Feedback Incorporation: Feedback, whether from peers, mentors, or self-reflection, is a goldmine. Re-evaluation is a structured way to incorporate this feedback.
  - Feedback can shed light on blind spots or areas of improvement.
  - It can validate efforts, showing areas where one excels.

Both continual learning and re-evaluation are iterative processes that feed into each other. As individuals learn, they gain new insights about themselves and the world, prompting re-evaluation. Conversely, re-evaluation might highlight areas that need further learning. Together, they ensure personal and professional growth that's responsive to the changing dynamics of our world.

Chapter 11: Living Your Purpose Daily

The discovery of one's life purpose is undoubtedly a transformative and exhilarating moment. It's like finding a compass in a vast wilderness, pointing you towards a path that feels intrinsically right.

However, the real challenge and reward lie not just in the discovery but in living out that purpose each day. It's one thing to understand your calling, but it's entirely another to integrate it into the rhythm of daily life, allowing it to shape decisions, guide actions, and infuse moments with meaning.

In this chapter, we'll explore the practical aspects of embodying your purpose daily. How can you ensure that the clarity you've found doesn't get obscured by the humdrum or chaos of everyday life?

How can you create a life where your purpose isn't just an abstract idea but a tangible guide that influences everything from your career choices to your relationships and daily habits? Just as a boat needs constant steering to stay on course, living your purpose requires ongoing attention and effort. It's about building habits, making conscious choices, and occasionally, realigning when life takes unexpected turns.

Let's delve into the ways you can ensure that your purpose isn't just something you've found, but something you live, breathe, and express daily.

Integrating Your Purpose into Daily Routines

Incorporating one's life purpose into daily routines is a foundational step towards living a life of genuine fulfilment and alignment.

When purpose is not merely a lofty ideal, but a practical guideline infused into our day-to-day actions, it becomes a compass that continually directs us toward meaning and satisfaction. Here's how one can seamlessly integrate purpose into everyday life:

Mindful Beginnings:

Starting the day with a sense of purpose can set the tone for everything that follows.

Tips:

- Engage in a morning meditation focusing on your life's purpose.
- Visualize your day aligning with this purpose.
- Write down a purpose-driven goal for the day in a journal.

Aligning Work with Purpose:

Many hours are spent working, so it's vital that our professional endeavors echo our life's purpose.

Tips:

- Identify tasks that directly correlate with your purpose and prioritize them.
- If possible, delegate or reduce tasks that are misaligned with your purpose.
- Take short breaks during work to realign and remind yourself of why you do what you do.

Purposeful Interactions:

Relationships and interactions provide ample opportunities to embody and reflect our purpose.

Tips:

- Listen actively, ensuring your communications resonate with your core values.
- Seek out collaborations or partnerships that synergize with your purpose.
- Use conflicts or challenges as opportunities to reaffirm and clarify your purpose.

End-of-Day Reflections:

Concluding the day by revisiting our purpose helps in embedding it deeper into our consciousness.

Tips:

- Dedicate a few minutes before sleep to reflect on how your day aligned with your purpose.
- Celebrate small victories that moved you closer to your life's mission.

- Identify areas of improvement or realignment for the next day.

Integrating Purpose into Leisure:

Even during downtime or leisure activities, there are opportunities to reinforce one's purpose.

Tips:

- Choose hobbies or activities that resonate with or complement your purpose.
- Engage in community service or philanthropy that aligns with your mission.
- Read books or consume content that deepens your understanding and connection to your purpose.

Physical Wellness and Purpose:

Maintaining physical health can significantly aid in fulfilling our life's purpose.

Tips:

- Choose exercises or routines that not only keep you fit but also mentally aligned, like yoga or nature walks.
- Understand that a healthy body can be a vessel to achieve your life's goals and act in harmony with your purpose.

In essence, the key lies not in making grand gestures but in subtly weaving purpose into the very fabric of our daily existence.

By consciously integrating our life's mission into mundane routines, we transform ordinary moments into extraordinary opportunities for growth, fulfilment, and purpose-driven living.

Setting Goals Aligned with Your Purpose

Finding and understanding your life's purpose is a monumental step in personal development. However, the journey doesn't end there. Once you've identified your purpose, the real work begins in aligning your everyday actions and long-term goals with that purpose.

Setting goals that reflect your purpose ensures that you remain on a path that resonates with your core values and aspirations.

Purpose-driven Clarity:

- Relevance: Goals aligned with your purpose tend to be more relevant and meaningful. This means that even when you encounter challenges, your intrinsic motivation remains strong.
- Direction: Knowing your purpose offers a clear direction. This clarity allows you to set goals that advance your larger mission, rather than diverting you from it.

The S.M.A.R.T. Approach:

- Specific: Be precise about what you want to achieve. If your purpose involves helping others, determine who you want to help and how.
- Measurable: Attach metrics or clear indicators of progress to your goals. For instance, if your purpose-driven goal is to educate

underprivileged children, a measurable target might be to tutor 20 kids by year-end.

- Achievable: Ensure that while your goals challenge you, they are still within realistic bounds. Overly ambitious goals can lead to burnout.

- Relevant: This is especially crucial for purpose-driven goals. Every goal you set should resonate with your bigger purpose.

- Time-bound: Assign deadlines to your goals. This provides motivation and allows you to track progress effectively.

Embrace Flexibility:

- Evolution: As you grow, both personally and professionally, your understanding of your purpose might evolve. It's essential to allow your goals to evolve with you.

- Check-ins: Regularly revisit your goals to ensure they still align with your purpose. Monthly or quarterly check-ins can be beneficial.

Seek Alignment in Every Aspect:

- Daily Tasks: Even daily to-do lists should, in some way, reflect your larger purpose-driven goals. If your purpose revolves around environmental sustainability, even a task as simple as 'buying groceries' can align with this by opting for sustainable products.

- Long-term Vision: Your long-term objectives, be it a 5-year or 10-year plan, should be a more magnified reflection of your purpose. If your purpose is about community building, a long-term goal might be to establish community canters in multiple neighbourhoods.

Seek Support and Collaboration:

- Mentors and Coaches: They can offer guidance, especially when you're unsure about aligning specific goals with your broader purpose.

- Community: Surrounding yourself with like-minded individuals or communities can provide external validation and support. Engaging in discussions can also offer fresh perspectives on goal alignment.

Ultimately, aligning your goals with your purpose is an ongoing process. It requires introspection, adaptability, and persistence.

By ensuring this alignment, not only do you make your goals more meaningful, but you also amplify the satisfaction and fulfilment derived from achieving them.

Inspirational Stories of Those Who Live Their Purpose Every Day

Steve Jobs: Merging Technology with Artistry

Steve Jobs, co-founder of Apple, lived his purpose daily by seeking to make a dent in the universe. His passion wasn't just for technology but for the intersection of technology with the humanities and arts.

From the inception of Apple in a garage to the introduction of revolutionary products like the iPhone, Jobs relentlessly pursued his vision of democratizing technology.

His iconic Stanford commencement speech, where he emphasized the importance of love and loss, of "connecting the dots," and of "staying hungry, staying foolish," further demonstrates the depth with which he approached life.

Jobs believed in challenging the status quo and not settling until the job was done perfectly. His daily drive wasn't just about creating products, but about crafting tools that could change the way humans interact, work, and express themselves.

Mahatma Gandhi: The Power of Non-Violence

Mahatma Gandhi, known as the father of the Indian nation, demonstrated the immense power of non-violence and civil disobedience in achieving profound societal change.

Gandhi's purpose was clear: to attain India's independence from British rule. However, it was the way he pursued this goal that set him apart. Eschewing violence, Gandhi believed in "Satyagraha" or the "force of truth." Through peaceful means, like the Salt March, he challenged oppressive laws and awakened a sense of national identity among millions. But his purpose wasn't merely political.

He advocated for self-reliance, communal harmony, and championed the cause of the downtrodden. Every action, every fast, every march, and every word he spoke was imbued with his purpose of creating a just, inclusive, and free India.

Oprah Winfrey: Empowering Voices

From her humble beginnings to becoming a media mogul, Oprah Winfrey's journey is a testament to resilience, empathy, and purpose-driven living. Oprah's purpose has consistently been to uplift, empower, and provide a platform for voices that often go unheard.

Through her iconic television show, she not only entertained but educated, shedding light on critical social issues, personal struggles, and tales of hope. Off-screen, her endeavors, like the Oprah Winfrey Leadership Academy for Girls in South Africa, showcase her commitment to empowering the next generation.

Every interview, story, and project Oprah undertake echoes her belief in the power of shared narratives and the potential for positive change.

Richard Branson: Business as a Force for Good

Entrepreneur Richard Branson, founder of the Virgin Group, is often recognized for his adventurous spirit and flair for disruption. While his business ventures span diverse sectors, from music to airlines to space travel, they are united by Branson's purpose of utilizing business as a force for good.

Branson believes that businesses should be about more than just making money; they should positively impact society and the planet. Through initiatives like The Elders, a group of global leaders working for peace and human rights, and the Virgin Earth Challenge, which sought solutions for climate change, Branson demonstrates his commitment to making a tangible difference. Each new venture and challenge he undertakes is a reflection of his ethos of blending profit with purpose.

Maya Angelou: A Symphony of Words and Wisdom

Maya Angelou, a gifted storyteller and writer, endured a tumultuous childhood filled with trauma and racial prejudice. Yet, her purpose was undeterred — to empower the silenced with her voice. Through her seminal work "I Know Why the Caged Bird Sings,"

Angelou confronted the demons of her past, shedding light on issues of racism, rape, identity, and literacy. Her words, spoken or written, consistently aimed at elevating the human spirit, promoting love, tolerance, and understanding.

Every lecture she delivered, every poem she penned, resonated with her purpose to inspire hope and resilience in the face of adversity.

Ratan Tata: Business Beyond Profits

Ratan Tata, an iconic figure in the Indian industrial landscape, helmed the Tata Group — one of India's largest conglomerates. Beyond his business acumen, Tata's approach was always purpose-driven, emphasizing societal welfare and ethical practices.

The Tata Trusts, under his leadership, have been instrumental in several philanthropic ventures in India, ranging from healthcare and education to rural development and social welfare. For Ratan Tata, every business decision weighed profit against the greater good.

His leadership highlighted that true success in business is not just about financial growth but also about uplifting and giving back to society.

Helen Keller: Triumph over Adversity

Helen Keller's life is a testament to the human spirit's indomitable will. Stricken by an illness as an infant, Keller lost both her sight and hearing, plunging her into a world of silence and darkness.

Yet, with the guidance of her teacher Anne Sullivan, she not only learned to communicate but also became a global ambassador for people with disabilities. Keller's purpose evolved into advocating for the blind and the deaf, striving for their education, employment, and rights.

Her daily life was a demonstration of sheer resilience, proving that physical disabilities couldn't confine one's potential or dreams.

Sir Edmund Hillary: Beyond the Summit

While Sir Edmund Hillary is globally renowned for being the first, along with Tenzing Norgay, to summit Mount Everest, his purpose transcended this monumental achievement.

Hillary dedicated much of his life to the welfare of the Sherpa people of Nepal. Recognizing the challenges faced by these high-altitude inhabitants, Hillary established the Himalayan Trust, which focused on building schools, hospitals, and infrastructure in the remote regions of the Himalayas.

His every expedition, lecture, and fundraising effort echoed his commitment to uplift the lives of the Sherpa community, highlighting that the real purpose often lies beyond personal achievements.

Frida Kahlo: Pain into Passion

Frida Kahlo, the iconic Mexican painter, turned personal anguish and physical pain into profound art. Having suffered from polio as a child and later enduring a horrific bus accident, Kahlo's life was marked by physical suffering and emotional tumult.

Yet, she transformed her pain into a passionate exploration of identity, post-colonialism, gender, class, and race in Mexican society. Each stroke of her brush was imbued with purpose, challenging societal norms and expressing raw, unfiltered emotion.

Through her artwork, Kahlo communicated a profound message about resilience, strength, and the power of self-expression.

Muhammad Yunus: Banking for the People

Dr. Muhammad Yunus, an economist from Bangladesh, envisioned a banking system that served the poor, a stark contrast to traditional banking mechanisms.

With the establishment of the Grameen Bank, Yunus introduced the concept of microcredit, providing small loans to impoverished entrepreneurs without requiring collateral.

His purpose was clear: alleviate poverty by empowering the underprivileged to become self-sufficient.

For his innovative approach to finance and profound impact on poverty reduction, Yunus was awarded the Nobel Peace Prize in 2006. His life's work stands as a testament to the power of innovative solutions tailored to address specific societal needs.

Chapter 12: The Ever-evolving Nature of Purpose

Many embark on the quest to find their life's purpose with the anticipation of stumbling upon a fixed, unchanging answer—a North Star that will guide them unerringly through every twist and turn of life.

Yet, just as we evolve with time, gaining new experiences, facing unique challenges, and growing in countless ways, so does our purpose.

It isn't static, cemented into the foundation of our being, but rather it's fluid, adaptable, and deeply intertwined with our life's journey.

This chapter delves into the dynamic nature of purpose. We'll explore why and how our purpose might shift over time, the factors contributing to its evolution, and most importantly, how to navigate and embrace these changes.

Far from being a sign of indecision or inconsistency, an evolving purpose can be a testament to growth, deeper self-awareness, and a richer, more layered life experience.

Stan Barren

The Possibility of Your Purpose Evolving or Changing Over Time

The notion of a life's purpose often brings to mind an enduring, unchanging mission, echoing the age-old quest for a singular destiny or calling. However, just as we evolve in our tastes, preferences, and understandings, our sense of purpose is equally susceptible to transformation. In fact, it's entirely natural for our purpose to shift, refine, or even completely change as we journey through the various stages of life.

One of the driving forces behind an evolving purpose is our continuous growth and accumulation of experiences. As we age, we don't merely add years to our life but also a plethora of experiences — successes, failures, joys, sorrows, discoveries, and realizations.

Each of these experiences molds our perspective, influences our desires, and consequently reshapes our sense of purpose. For instance, a person dedicated to climbing corporate ladders in their 20s might find a deep-seated desire to teach or mentor by the time they reach their 40s, having understood the value of imparting knowledge.

Furthermore, our environments and the societal structures we're embedded in are in a state of flux. Technological advances, socio-political changes, and even global crises can radically alter our worldview.

Such external shifts can instigate a re-evaluation of what feels meaningful to us. For example, many have found new purposes in environmental or social causes, driven by the alarming changes they see in the world around them.

It's also worth noting that our internal world — our values, beliefs, and aspirations — isn't static. Personal revelations or profound moments of introspection can lead to a recalibration of what we deem significant.

A life-altering event, like a health scare or the birth of a child, might cause someone to prioritize health and family over previously held ambitions, leading to a shift in their life's purpose.

The idea that purpose can change is liberating. It frees us from the pressure of finding that one 'true' calling, allowing for exploration, mistakes, and growth. Instead of feeling anchored to a singular purpose identified early in life, we can embrace the dynamism of our journey, understanding that each phase might come with its own unique sense of purpose.

By doing so, we ensure that our purpose remains aligned with our most authentic self, making our pursuits feel both meaningful and fulfilling.

Navigating Transitions and Shifts in Purpose

In the quest to unearth one's life purpose, it's crucial to recognize that purpose is not always a static entity. Like rivers carving new paths through landscapes, our purposes too may evolve, reroute, or deepen based on myriad life experiences.

Just as we grow and change, so might the things that drive and inspire us. However, navigating these transitions and shifts in purpose can be both challenging and enriching. Transitions in life, such as changes in career, personal losses, new relationships, or even transformative experiences like travel or education, can usher in shifts in how we perceive our life's purpose.

Sometimes, what we believed was our driving force in our twenties might feel less compelling in our forties. This is natural. As we accumulate experiences, our understanding of the world and ourselves refines, and with it, our sense of purpose might take on a new dimension or direction.

Handling these shifts requires a blend of introspection, patience, and adaptability. It's essential not to view these changes as regressions or failures. Instead, they are a testament to our growth and the multifaceted nature of human existence.

One should be cautious, however, to differentiate between a genuine evolution in purpose and transient feelings of doubt or fear. The former is a deep-seated realization, while the latter might be fleeting, stemming from external pressures or temporary setbacks.

A vital aspect of navigating these transitions is open dialogue. Discussing feelings, uncertainties, or newfound passions with trusted friends, mentors, or counsellors can offer clarity. They can act as mirrors, reflecting perspectives we might overlook.

At the same time, giving oneself the permission to explore, take risks, and even make mistakes is integral. After all, it's in the act of journeying through the myriad terrains of life that we often stumble upon our most profound purposes.

In the end, it's beneficial to approach shifts in purpose as opportunities—chances to delve deeper into our souls, to reinvent, and to embrace the vast spectrum of passions and callings that life offers. By understanding that purpose is an evolving journey rather than a fixed destination, we can navigate its shifts with grace, curiosity, and optimism.

Conclusion

As we draw near the end of our exploration into finding life's purpose, it's essential to recognize that the journey itself offers insights and revelations that are just as meaningful as the destination.

The "Conclusion" section is not just a summary of what we've discussed; rather, it's an invitation for reflection and an urging towards future action. It encapsulates the essence of our discourse and serves as a compass for those moments when you might find yourself adrift.

Whether you've found clarity or are still meandering through the maze of self-discovery, this concluding segment is designed to anchor, inspire, and reinvigorate your pursuit.

Embark on Your Journey

There is an old adage that says, "The journey of a thousand miles begins with a single step." This couldn't be truer when it comes to discovering your life's purpose. Often, the mere act of beginning, of taking that initial step, can be the most daunting.

However, once taken, it propels you forward into a realm of self-discovery, personal growth, and fulfilment. Your life's purpose isn't a destination; it's a continuous journey.

Recognize the Imperative:

- Every individual possesses a unique combination of experiences, skills, and passions. This unique blend equips you with a singular perspective that the world needs.
- By not embarking on this journey, you're not only doing a disservice to yourself but potentially to the world that could benefit from your gifts.

Start Small:

- You don't have to make life-altering decisions or huge leaps immediately. Remember, even the smallest step in the right direction counts.
- Activities like journaling, meditation, or simply setting aside ten minutes a day for introspection can be starting points.

Seek Support:

- Share your journey with friends, family, or even a support group. Surrounding yourself with a supportive community can provide encouragement, accountability, and different perspectives.
- Consider seeking a mentor or coach who can provide guidance, or join workshops and seminars that align with your exploration.

Stay Open and Curious:

- As you start, you may face more questions than answers. That's okay. It's essential to remain open-minded and treat every experience as a learning opportunity.
- Embrace the unknown, and don't be disheartened by setbacks or detours. They are all a part of the journey.

Commit to Consistency:

- The journey to find purpose isn't a one-time event. It's a continuous process of growth, understanding, and realignment.
- Dedicate time regularly to reflect, reassess, and recommit to your path.

Now, with these pointers in mind, I urge you, dear reader, to take a moment. Reflect on where you are and where you wish to be. Understand that your purpose is a compass, guiding you through life's maze, providing direction and meaning.

And like any grand expedition, it's the journey, the challenges faced, the lessons learned, and the growth experienced that make it truly fulfilling. So, why wait? Embark on your journey today. Your purpose awaits.

The Journey and the Destination: Equal Pillars of Purpose

In our relentless quest to find purpose, we often become fixated on the end goal – that clear, unshakeable purpose that will give meaning to our existence. However, it's crucial to understand that purpose is not just a destination, a final point we arrive at.

Instead, the journey towards uncovering that purpose is equally significant. Every step we take, every setback we face, every moment of enlightenment – these are the experiences that shape us, and they hold immense value in our overall narrative of purpose.

The journey, filled with its trials and tribulations, is where the true metamorphosis happens. As we navigate the labyrinth of self-discovery, we shed outdated beliefs, challenge ingrained norms, and confront our deepest fears.

This transformative process allows us to understand not just our destination but also the why and how of our pursuit. In many ways, the journey itself is a reflection of our resilience, adaptability, and commitment to growth.

Moreover, while a destination provides clarity, the journey offers invaluable lessons. It's during the voyage that we learn patience, persistence, and the power of introspection.

These skills and insights mold our character, ensuring that once we do recognize our purpose, we have the wisdom and fortitude to live it out authentically.

Furthermore, it's essential to recognize that our understanding of our purpose might evolve over time. What we perceive as our ultimate goal at one life stage may shift as we grow and gather more experiences.

Hence, if we only value the destination, we might find ourselves in a state of perpetual dissatisfaction. But by valuing the journey, we cultivate a mindset of continual growth, understanding, and self-appreciation, irrespective of the evolving nature of our purpose.

In essence, while the destination gives our journey direction, it's the journey itself that enriches us. Both facets are intertwined in the intricate dance of life, where the path travelled holds as much significance as the endpoint.

To truly embrace our purpose, we must learn to cherish every step, every challenge, and every revelation along the way. For in the end, the journey and the destination are but two sides of the same coin of purpose, each lending value to the other.

Appendices

In our journey to uncover life's purpose, understanding the theory and immersing ourselves in introspective narratives is just the beginning. The real transformation often emerges from active engagement, from putting pen to paper, and challenging our internal paradigms.

The appendices, therefore, are more than just supplementary material. Think of them as a toolkit, a compass, guiding you through the intricate maze of self-discovery.

Here, you will find an array of practical exercises, worksheets, and resources meticulously curated to complement each chapter of this guide. They are designed to provide you with a hands-on approach to understanding and defining your unique purpose.

Alongside, a recommended reading list awaits the insatiable reader, offering deeper dives into topics touched upon in the book. Moreover, for those seeking communal exploration or expert guidance, a list of online platforms and communities dedicated to exploring life's purpose is provided.

Dive into these tools with an open heart and mind. They are meant to be revisited, reflected upon, and even shared with others on the same path. Let this be your tangible guidepost, helping you navigate the intangible dimensions of purpose and passion.

Additional Exercises and Worksheets

Mind Mapping Your Interests

1. Mind mapping is a visual tool that helps you organize and analyse your thoughts.
2. Begin with a central idea (like "My Life's Purpose") and branch out with associated ideas, interests, and passions.
   - This can highlight intersections of interests that may hint at a deeper purpose.
   - Use colours, symbols, or images to make connections more vivid.

The 5 Whys Technique

1. Rooted in problem-solving methodologies, asking "why" repeatedly helps get to the core reason behind a thought or feeling.
2. Start with a simple statement about something you enjoy or feel strongly about.
   - For example: "I enjoy helping others."
   - Ask "Why?" and jot down the answer.
   - Repeat the "Why?" question for the answer, up to five times or until you reach a profound realization about its root cause.

The Role Model Analysis

1. Consider the people you admire, whether they're historical figures, celebrities, family members, or colleagues.

2. Write down their names and list the specific qualities or actions you admire.

- This can give insight into values you hold dear, or aspirations you have for yourself.
- Analyse patterns among these figures. Are there commonalities in their paths or traits?

Journal Prompts for Purpose

1. Daily or weekly journaling can unearth deep feelings and insights about one's purpose.
2. Some prompts to consider:

- "When was the last time I felt truly alive and what was I doing?"
- "If money were no object, what would I do with my time?"
- "What are the common themes in the moments of my life that brought the most joy or fulfilment?"
- "Describe a time when you faced a challenge but felt that the struggle was worth it. Why?"

Skill and Talent Inventory

1. An objective look at your skills can sometimes hint at areas where your purpose might lie.
2. List all skills and talents, from the mundane to the impressive.

- Next, categorize them: Which do you enjoy most? Which do you feel most proud of?

Which have the most significant impact on others?

- Look for overlaps in these categories for clues about your purpose.

The Legacy Exercise

1. A forward-thinking activity where you envision the legacy you'd like to leave behind.
2. Answer prompts such as:
   - "If someone were to write a biography about me, what would I want it to say?"
   - "What do I want to be remembered for?"
   - Reflecting on the end goal can sometimes illuminate the path you'd like to take.

Values Clarification Exercise

1. Understanding your core values is instrumental in recognizing what drives you.
2. List out various values (e.g., integrity, family, knowledge, wealth, health).
   - Rank them based on their importance to you.
   - Reflect on the top 5. Ask yourself why they are so crucial and how they manifest in your life.

Dream Day Visualization

1. A guided meditation or visualization exercise can help you imagine your ideal day.

2. Close your eyes and picture a day where everything goes perfectly, from morning to night.
   - What are you doing? Who are you with? How do you feel?
   - Jot down the details after your visualization. These insights might give clues about your desires and aspirations.

Personal SWOT Analysis

1. A SWOT Analysis, commonly used in businesses, stands for Strengths, Weaknesses, Opportunities, and Threats.
2. Apply this analysis to yourself.
   - List out your strengths and how you can capitalize on them.
   - Acknowledge your weaknesses and consider ways to mitigate or improve them.
   - Identify opportunities you can seize and potential threats or obstacles.
   - By evaluating yourself in this structured manner, you can align your purpose with realistic goals and strategies.

Life's Highs and Lows Chart

1. By visualizing your life's significant events, you can discern patterns or pivotal moments.
2. Plot out your life's highs and lows on a timeline.

- Next to each event, write a brief note about why it was a high or low point.
- Reflect on the factors or decisions that led to these moments. This can help pinpoint recurring themes or values in your life.

Future Self Letter

1. Writing a letter to your future self can be a profound exercise in understanding your current values and hopes.
2. Pen down a letter addressing your future self-5 or 10 years from now.

   - Mention your current state, your hopes, fears, dreams, and questions you might have.
   - Revisit this letter in the future to gauge your growth and the evolution of your purpose.

Purpose Statement Crafting

1. After undertaking multiple exercises, try to craft a concise statement that encapsulates your life's purpose.
2. Use the insights gathered to write a 1-2 sentence purpose statement.

   - This serves as a guiding beacon, helping you make decisions aligned with your larger goals.
   - Regularly revisit and refine this statement as you evolve.

Engaging with these exercises isn't a one-time affair. It's beneficial to revisit them periodically. As you grow and evolve, your perspectives may shift, and these tools can continually offer fresh insights.

Remember, the journey to find purpose is ongoing, and it's as much about understanding oneself as it is about defining a clear life direction.

Recommended Reading List

Reading is one of the most powerful ways to gain insight into the human experience, especially when it comes to understanding one's purpose in life.

The following list includes an array of books, from philosophical classics to contemporary self-help, that have illuminated the path for countless individuals on their quest for purpose.

"Man's Search for Meaning" by Viktor E. Frankl:

One of the most profound books ever written on the subject of purpose, this autobiographical account by Viktor Frankl narrates his experiences in Nazi concentration camps.

A psychiatrist by profession, Frankl introduces "logotherapy," emphasizing that life has potential meaning under any conditions, even the most brutal ones. His reflections delve deep into the heart of human existence and the innate search for purpose.

"The Alchemist" by Paulo Coelho:

This allegorical novel is an enchanting story about a shepherd named Santiago who embarks on a journey to discover his personal legend.

Through Santiago's adventures, Coelho beautifully elucidates the universal human quest for purpose and the importance of listening to our hearts.

"Drive: The Surprising Truth About What Motivates Us" by Daniel H. Pink:

Pink challenges the traditional thinking about motivation and purpose. Drawing from vast amounts of scientific research, he argues that autonomy, mastery, and purpose are the key factors driving deep satisfaction in both personal and professional realms.

"The Path: What Chinese Philosophers Can Teach Us About the Good Life" by Michael Puett & Christine Gross-Loh:

This book dives deep into the teachings of Chinese philosophers, offering refreshing insights into leading a purposeful life. It challenges Western perceptions about well-being and success, suggesting that small changes in daily routines can lead to profound transformations.

"Start with Why: How Great Leaders Inspire Everyone to Take Action" by Simon Sinek:

Sinek explores the idea that successful individuals and organizations operate on a simple principle: they understand their "why." By identifying and articulating a clear purpose, these entities can inspire action, drive change, and achieve lasting success.

"Big Magic: Creative Living Beyond Fear" by Elizabeth Gilbert:

A delightful read for anyone looking to find purpose through creativity. Gilbert, author of "Eat, Pray, Love," delves into the intricacies of the creative process, encouraging readers to embrace curiosity, let go of fear, and uncover their unique path in life.

"Daring Greatly: How the Courage to Be Vulnerable Transforms the Way We Live, Love, Parent, and Lead" by Brené Brown:

Brown's ground-breaking research on vulnerability, shame, and empathy offers invaluable insights into leading a purpose-driven life.

The book underscores the idea that embracing vulnerability can lead to richer, more purposeful relationships and experiences.

"The Purpose Driven Life: What on Earth Am I Here For?" by Rick Warren:

A spiritual classic, Warren's book offers a day-by-day guide to uncovering God's purpose for our lives. Written from a Christian perspective, it addresses profound questions about existence, significance, and purpose, guiding readers through a 40-day personal spiritual journey.

"Flow: The Psychology of Optimal Experience" by Mihaly Csikszentmihalyi:

Csikszentmihalyi introduces the concept of 'flow' – a state of complete immersion and heightened focus in an activity.

The book delves into how achieving this state consistently can lead to a life filled with meaning and happiness, thus emphasizing the role of purposeful activities in our lives.

"The Power of Now: A Guide to Spiritual Enlightenment" by Eckhart Tolle:

Tolle's masterpiece discusses the importance of living in the present moment and freeing oneself from the shackles of ego-driven thinking. While it doesn't address 'purpose' directly, understanding and internalizing the book's teachings can lead to a more profound, purposeful existence by transcending superficial pursuits.

"Finding Your Own North Star: Claiming the Life You Were Meant to Live" by Martha Beck:

Beck offers a step-by-step program to help readers discover their own unique, inborn nature, and then use that knowledge to shape a life filled with purpose. Drawing from her experiences as a life coach, she provides tools and exercises to navigate life's challenges and transitions.

"The Element: How Finding Your Passion Changes Everything" by Ken Robinson:

Sir Ken Robinson, an influential voice in education, delves into how discovering the intersection of passion and natural talent can lead to a fulfilling and purposeful life. Using real-life examples, the book illustrates how identifying one's 'element' can transform their life.

"Awaken the Giant Within: How to Take Immediate Control of Your Mental, Emotional, Physical and Financial Destiny!" by Tony Robbins:

Robbins, a renowned life coach, provides strategies and techniques for mastering emotions, finances, relationships, and life. The book emphasizes the importance of taking action and steering one's life towards its intended purpose.

"Ikigai: The Japanese Secret to a Long and Happy Life" by Héctor García and Francesc Miralles:

Rooted in Japanese culture, 'ikigai' translates to 'reason for being.' The book delves into the age-old wisdom from Okinawa, a Japanese region known for its high number of centenarians. It provides insights into finding one's 'ikigai' and living a life filled with joy and purpose.

About the Author

Stan Barren is a motivational writer and coach with a deeply ingrained philosophy: every challenge faced is an opportunity for growth. Born in a small town, his early life was marked by determination and perseverance. Stan's academic journey was briefly nurtured at a university. However, financial constraints led him to leave prematurely, two exams shy of completion.

Despite the setback and lacking a formal college degree, Stan navigated the labyrinth of life with tenacity. He took on an array of jobs in the subsequent years, building resilience with each step. Married young, he faced the ebbs and flows of life, confronting moments where he was jobless, financially strained, and close to losing everything.

Yet, through these trials, Stan's unwavering optimism never dimmed. He always sought the proverbial rainbow after every storm, believing that his challenges were life's way of forging his character.

An avid reader and writer since high school, Stan's passion for personal growth never waned. He ardently delved into the world of personal development, making the most of free resources at libraries and online platforms. His insights, born from personal experiences and relentless self-study, became the foundation for his motivational work.

Today, Stan is indebted to life's teachings and feels a profound responsibility to give back. He believes that by inspiring and uplifting others, he inches closer to realizing his own dreams. His life's mission revolves around the essence of hope, resilience, and the transformative power of a positive mindset.